SIX MORE MINIATURES

Half-a-Dozen Fifteen-Minute Comedies

By
DAN SUTHERLAND

To
KOBI

SAMUEL   FRENCH

LONDON
NEW YORK   TORONTO   SYDNEY   HOLLYWOOD

Copyright © 19514 by Samuel French Ltd
All Rights Reserved

SIX MORE MINATURES is fully protected under the copyright laws of the British Commonwealth, including Canada, the United States of America, and all other countries of the Copyright Union. All rights, including professional and amateur stage productions, recitation, lecturing, public reading, motion picture, radio broadcasting, television and the rights of translation into foreign languages are strictly reserved.

ISBN 978-0-573-00017-1

www.samuelfrench.co.uk
www.samuelfrench.com

For Amateur Production Enquiries

United Kingdom and World excluding North America

plays@samuelfrench.co.uk

020 7255 4302/01

Each title is subject to availability from Samuel French, depending upon country of performance.

CAUTION: Professional and amateur producers are hereby warned that SIX MORE MINATURES is subject to a licensing fee. Publication of this play does not imply availability for performance. Both amateurs and professionals considering a production are strongly advised to apply to the appropriate agent before starting rehearsals, advertising, or booking a theatre. A licensing fee must be paid whether the title is presented for charity or gain and whether or not admission is charged.

The professional rights in this play are controlled by Samuel French Ltd, 24-32 Stephenson Way, London, NW1 2HD.

No one shall make any changes in this title for the purpose of production. No part of this book may be reproduced, stored in a retrieval system, or transmitted in any form, by any means, now known or yet to be invented, including mechanical, electronic, photocopying, recording, videotaping, or otherwise, without the prior written permission of the publisher. No one shall upload this title, or part of this title, to any social media websites.

The right of Dan Sutherland to be identified as author of this work has been asserted in accordance with Section 77 of the Copyright, Designs and Patents Act 1988.

CONTENTS

		page
1.	THE CLEAN UP F. 2	1
2.	TRYING TO TAKE THINGS QUIETLY M: 1. F: 2	17
3.	SCHERZO IN TWO FLATS M: 1. F: 2	33
4.	FATHER'S ECONOMY DRIVE M: 1. F: 3	49
5.	ART FOR ART'S SAKE M: 1. F: 3	65
6.	THE MAN WHO UNDERSTOOD WOMEN M: 2. F: 4	81

THE CLEAN UP

CHARACTERS

LIZ } office cleaners
DOLLY

The action of the play passes in the offices of Millibank and Co. Ltd, general importers, early one morning before office hours

THE CLEAN UP*

Scene—*The offices of Millibank and Co. Ltd, general importers. Early one morning before office hours.*
It is a small office with a door c *of the back wall and a window* r. *A desk and chair stand* rc. *On the desk there is a typewriter, a telephone and a filing basket of copy letters. A waste-paper basket, half-filled with discarded papers, stands below the desk. There is a filing cabinet* l. *Other suitable dressing may be added at the discretion of the producer.*
(See the Ground Plan at the end of the play)

When the Curtain *rises,* Liz, *an office cleaner, is on her knees* c, *washing the floor. She is in her late forties, and wears a nondescript dark dress, a grubby apron and a man's flat cap pinned to her wispy grey hair. As she scrubs she sings, her voice straining a little as she reaches for the most distant places.*

Liz (*singing*)
    All the birds of the air started sighing and a-sobbin',
    When they heard of the death of poor Cock Robin,
    When they heard of the death o-of poo-or Cock——

    (Dolly *enters. She is much the same as Liz in general get-up and appearance*)

Dolly (*as she enters*) Finished, ducks? (*She crosses to* r *of Liz*)
Liz (*completing the song*) —Robin.
Dolly. Eh?
Liz (*speaking*) Cock Robin.
Dolly. What about 'im?
Liz. 'E's dead. (*She wipes the floor in front of her and drops the cloth and brush into the bucket*)
Dolly (*concerned*) Go on—is 'e? Tch! The way people are dying these days—makes you think.

* See page iv.

LIZ. You finished?
DOLLY. Nigh on. Only got the passage to do.
LIZ (*rising*) Well, I don't want to say nothing, but some people don't 'arf get round fast.
DOLLY. You're not insinuating anything, are you, dear?
LIZ. 'Oo, me?
DOLLY. Because if you are, let me tell you Mr Millibank could eat 'is dinner off of 'is office floor.
LIZ. Judging by the looks of 'im, that's probably just what 'e does do.
DOLLY. I bet 'e ain't thinking about eating today—what with the burglary 'ere yesterday and everything.
LIZ. D'you know what the night watchman told me?
DOLLY. No, what?
LIZ. 'E said they took five thousand pounds. Made a proper muck of the safe, they did. 'Ave you seen it?
DOLLY. Seen it? Didn't they leave me to clear up all the mess after the police 'ad gone? Proper muck *they* made, too—great big feet all over everything.
LIZ. Got in during the night, didn't they?
DOLLY. What, the policemen's feet?
LIZ. No—the burglars.
DOLLY. Through the front door, too, so they told me.
LIZ. I bet old Millibank wasn't 'arf wild.
DOLLY. Proper tearing 'is 'air, 'e was.
LIZ. What there is of it.
DOLLY. I don't like 'im, you know.
LIZ. No, nor me. Nasty type, if ever I saw one.
DOLLY. Yes, and you've seen plenty of nasty types in your time, 'aven't you, dear? You married two of them.
LIZ. Coming from you, 'aving seen your 'Arry . . .
DOLLY. 'E said to me the other day, 'e said, "Mrs 'Uggins, I found two cigarette ends under the radiator".
DOLLY. Cor, did 'e reely? What did you say?
DOLLY. I said, "Well, Mr Millibank," I said, "if you will go crawling about the office on your 'ands and knees", I said, "you must expect to find funny things in funny places."

Liz. And what did 'e say to that?
Dolly. Couldn't think of a thing. Stopped 'im dead, it did. But then, I always was good with repart.
Liz. With what, dear?
Dolly. Repart. You know—quick answers.
Liz. Oh.
Dolly. 'E's a nasty type, all right. I wouldn't put it past 'im to have faked this robbery.
Liz. What do you mean?
Dolly. Well, *pretend* there's been a burglary and take the money 'imself.
Liz. Coo—do you really think so?
Dolly. Well, it wouldn't be very 'ard, would it? I mean, 'e's got the keys of the building, 'asn't 'e? All 'e'd 'ave to do would be to come back after everyone 'ad gone 'ome, break the safe open . . .
Liz. What with?
Dolly. Eh?
Liz. I said, what with?
Dolly. Oh, well—if you're going to argue . . .
Liz (*argumentatively*) I'm not arguing. I just want to know what 'e'd break the safe open with.
Dolly. Well, as a matter of fact, of course, 'e wouldn't *ave* to break it open. 'E's got the keys, 'asn't 'e?
Liz (*thoughtfully*) That's true.
Dolly. 'E could wear gloves. Probably did.
Liz. What for? It wasn't cold yesterday.
Dolly. Didn't you ever 'ave *no* education? All crooks wear gloves so as not to leave any fingerprints.
Liz. Oh. Well, what was the police doing looking all over the safe with magnifying glasses?
Dolly. Just in case 'e '*ad*.
Liz. But 'e was too smart for 'em?
Dolly. Of course. Bet 'e didn't leave a clue.
Liz (*admiringly*) Oh, 'e's clever, all right. Clean away with five thousand quid and everybody feeling sorry for 'im.
Dolly. That's right. Makes you sick, doesn't it?
Liz. I suppose it's our duty to tell the police reely.
Dolly. I suppose it is.

Liz. 'E shouldn't be allowed to get away with it.
Dolly. That's right.
Liz. I tell you one thing, though.
Dolly. What's that?
Liz. We'll 'ave to prove it.
Dolly. Why? It's obvious 'e done it, isn't it?
Liz. Course it is. But you know what the police are.
Dolly. Ah, that's right. No intelligence.
Liz. Not like us.
Dolly. No.
Liz. All right—let's prove it, then.
Dolly. All right. (*She pauses*) 'Ow?
Liz. Now, if you're going to make difficulties . . .
Dolly. Sorry.
Liz. Look, let's suppose the place is all shut up and everyone's gone 'ome——
Dolly. Yes.
Liz. —all the lights are out, you see——
Dolly. Yes.
Liz. —'e comes in the front door with 'is key——
Dolly. Yes.
Liz. —creeps upstairs——
Dolly (*getting enthralled*) Yes.
Liz. —looks round to see if there's anybody about . . .
Dolly. What, in the dark?
Liz. Ah, but supposing it wasn't dark? Suppose 'e turned the light on?
Dolly. Suppose 'e did?
Liz. Then he could see whether there was anyone 'ere or not, couldn't 'e?
Dolly. But I thought you said 'e waited till everybody 'ad gone 'ome?
Liz. Ah, that's what 'e *wanted* everyone to think.
Dolly. Why?
Liz. So that nobody would know 'e'd got a confederate inside.
Dolly. 'Ad 'e?
Liz. Must've 'ad. Otherwise what would 'e want to turn the lights on for?
Dolly. Oh. Well, 'oo was it?

LIZ. Can't you guess?
DOLLY. No.
LIZ. That secertry of 'is. Miss Babson. The one that sits 'ere.
DOLLY. You mean the one with fair 'air?
LIZ (*sniffing*) If you want to call it fair. Secertry! Huh!
DOLLY (*wisely*) I know what you mean. You mean . . .
LIZ (*sharply*) Now, there's no need to get vulgar.
DOLLY. Sorry.
LIZ. So 'im and this girl—they got the whole thing fixed up between them, see?
DOLLY (*shaking her head*) I don't like it, Dolly.
LIZ. Why not? Obvious, if you ask me. That girl—why she can't even type.
DOLLY. 'Ow do you know?
LIZ. Times out of number, when I've 'ad to clear out that there waste-paper basket, it's been full of letters she's messed up and 'ad to start again.
DOLLY. Go on?
LIZ. 'Sfact. Costs the company a fortune, she does.
DOLLY. She 'as now.
LIZ (*pointing to the waste-paper basket*) Look at that basket—full of paper she's wasted.
DOLLY. That reminds me—I 'aven't emptied it yet. (*She crosses to the waste-paper basket and takes some pieces of paper from it, including one piece of pink copy paper. She crosses to* R *of Liz and reads from the pieces*) "Dear *Tirs* . . ." Here's another one. (*She reads*) "We 'ave to acknowledge *deceipt* of your letter . . ." Cor! And look at this one. (*She reads*) "With reference to your *setter* of the twenty-fifth inst. . . ."
LIZ. 'Opeless.
DOLLY (*reading the pink piece of paper*) 'Ere—look at this one, on pink paper, too—gone proper barmy with this one. Listen. (*She reads*) "The quick brown fox jumps over the lazy dog—the quick brown fox jumps over the lazy dog—the quick brown fox jumps over the . . ."
LIZ (*mystified*) What? Let's 'ave a look.
DOLLY. 'Ere you are. (*She hands the piece of pink paper to Liz*)

(LIZ *crosses to* R *of the desk, stands with her back to the window and with furrowed brow studies the paper*)

LIZ (*reading*) "The quick brown fox . . ." I think she's nuts. "The quick brown fox . . ." (*An idea strikes her. She thumps the desk. Delightedly*) I've got it!
DOLLY. What?
LIZ (*crossing to* R *of Dolly*) It's a code.
DOLLY. A code? Do you mean a code in the doze?
LIZ. No, no. A code—like the thing spies use.
DOLLY (*round-eyed*) Do you think she's a spy?
LIZ. No—but crooks use codes, don't they?
DOLLY. Do they?
LIZ. Of course—like "Knock twice and ask for Charlie".
DOLLY. That's what my old man does when 'e goes round to the pub after closing time.
LIZ. This is a clue. Their 'ole guilt is writ on this paper.
DOLLY (*interested*) Is it? Let's 'ave another look. (*She takes the paper from Liz and reads*) "The quick brown fox . . ."
LIZ. No. It's a code, I tell you. It doesn't mean what it says there—it means something else.
DOLLY (*baffled*) I don't get it.
LIZ. Look—"The quick brown fox"—that's '*im*, see?
DOLLY. 'Oo?
LIZ. 'Im—Mr Millibank.
DOLLY. Well, I must admit 'e *is* a bit foxy, but . . .
LIZ. 'E's quick, isn't 'e?
DOLLY. Quick enough to say plenty when you sweep the dust under the rug in 'is office.
LIZ. And 'e's got brown 'air, 'asn't 'e?
DOLLY. What there is of it.
LIZ. So 'e's quick, and 'e's brown-'aired, and 'e's foxy. Right?
DOLLY. All right. But . . .
LIZ (*interrupting*) I know what you're going to say—'oo's the lazy dog?
DOLLY. That's right, I was.

Liz (*dramatically*) I 'eard 'im use those very words.
Dolly. You did? When?
Liz. Only the other day. 'E said, "If that lazy dog of a night watchman doesn't buck 'is ideas up, I'll fire 'im."
Dolly. You mean . . . ?
Liz. That's right. "Lazy dog" is code for old Tom.
Dolly. Coo! (*A thought strikes her*) But what does 'e want to jump over 'im for?
Liz (*dramatically*) That's code again—it means—*get in while old Tom isn't looking.*
Dolly. Liz, I believe you're right!
Liz. Of course I'm right.
Dolly. Got 'em red 'anded.
Liz. That's right.
Dolly. 'Ere—wait a minute. Why should she type it over and over again?
Liz. To impress it on 'er memory. That was the secret plan.
Dolly. I think you've been reading too many *Sexton Blakes*.
Liz. Look—there's been a burglary, 'asn't there?
Dolly. Yes, but . . .
Liz. And 'e took the money, didn't 'e?
Dolly. I suppose so.
Liz. And if 'e did, she was in it with 'im, wasn't she?
Dolly. Yes, but . . .
Liz (*indicating the paper*) And there's the plan all written down on pink paper in black and white. What are you arguing about?
Dolly. I'm not arguing. But . . .
Liz. Look, if I don't get any co-operation from you, I won't share the reward with you.
Dolly. The what?
Liz. The reward.
Dolly. What reward?
Liz. There's bound to be a reward—there always is.
Dolly. Coo! 'Ow much?
Liz. I don't know. Usually ten per cent, isn't it?
Dolly. What's ten per cent of five thousand quid?
Liz. Oh—er—er—'ere, give me a pencil. (*She sits at the*

desk, picks up a pencil and attempts to work out the amount. She chews the end of the pencil, counts on her fingers and scowls ferociously)

(DOLLY *stands over* Liz, *putting in a helpful word now and again*)

Multiply by . . . Divide by . . . Times ten—that's forty-three—put down nine . . .
DOLLY. And carry one.
LIZ. Eh?
DOLLY. Carry one.
LIZ. One what?
DOLLY. Carry *one*. Put down *one*.
LIZ. Oh. (*She returns to her figuring*) Carry one. Add thirteen—take away the number you first thought of. Yes, 'ere you are—seven 'undred and thirty-five pounds, nineteen and fourpence.
DOLLY. Is that ten per cent of five thousand quid?
LIZ. If you think you can do any better . . .
DOLLY (*hastily*) No, no. I'm sure you're right, dear.
LIZ. Over seven 'undred quid. Think what we can do with that.
DOLLY (*crossing to* C; *dreamily*) Five 'undred for me and two 'undred for you.
LIZ (*rising; sharply*) What? '*Ow* much for me?
DOLLY. Two 'undred.
LIZ. Two 'undred for *you*, you mean—the five 'undred is mine.
DOLLY. I found the paper.
LIZ. Yes, but I worked out what it meant.
DOLLY. If I 'adn't found it, you couldn't of worked it out.
LIZ. If I 'adn't of worked it out, you wouldn't of known what it meant.
DOLLY (*generously*) All right—I'll tell you what we'll do—let's split it in 'arf—three 'undred each.
LIZ (*crossing to Dolly*) Done. (*She shakes hands with* DOLLY, *then a thought strikes her*) 'Ere, wait **a minute—** we've lost a 'undred quid somewhere.

DOLLY. Why worry about a little thing like that when we've got all this money?
LIZ. You're right, Dolly—what's a 'undred quid?
DOLLY. I'll draw the reward and give you three 'undred . . .
LIZ. No—*I'll* draw the reward and give *you* three 'undred.
DOLLY (*flatly*) Oh.
LIZ (*dreamily*) I'll buy myself a new 'at——
DOLLY (*glancing at Liz's cap*) Not before it's wanted.
LIZ. —go to Southend for the day—'ave a winkle supper—take a day off from work——
DOLLY. You'll probably 'ave to after the winkle supper.
LIZ. —and I'll send young Alfie to the pictures and give 'im a tanner for sweets—no, a shilling.
DOLLY. Spendthrift!
LIZ. Well, just because you've got a lot of money that's no reason for throwing it around, is it?
DOLLY. You're throwing it around like a man with no arms. You've got through about two quid so far—(*she snaps her fingers*) just like that.
LIZ. What are you going to do with yours?
DOLLY. I'm going to 'ave a 'oliday in Italy.
LIZ. Italy? Whatever for?
DOLLY. I've always wanted to go on one of them boats on the canals—what do they call them—gorgonzolas.
LIZ. Oo, I wouldn't trust myself to them Italians—not with all that money on me.
DOLLY. That's all right, dear, I shall 'ave it stitched to my roll-ons.
LIZ (*reminiscently*) I went on a 'oliday once with Bert.
DOLLY. What 'appened?
LIZ. Nothing.
DOLLY (*sympathetically*) I know what you mean, dear—I've 'ad 'olidays like that meself.
LIZ. Sitting there on the front, we was, with the rain pouring down . . .
DOLLY. Yes, I know. But now we've got all this money . . .

Liz. 'Ere!
Dolly. What?
Liz. Suppose there isn't a reward?
Dolly. What! There must be.
Liz. Well, you never know.
Dolly. 'Ow can we find out?
Liz. Well, we can't ring up the police and ask 'em, can we?
Dolly. No, I suppose we can't.
Liz. I know—it'll be in the paper.
Dolly. What paper?
Liz. Any paper. It'll say, "Anybody giving information leading to the recovery of the stolen goods will be suitably rewarded".
Dolly (*admiringly*) 'Ow do you know all that?
Liz. It's my legal training.
Dolly. I didn't know you 'ad any.
Liz. Oh, yes—I used to clean a solicitor's office.
Dolly. Well, fancy that.
Liz. Go on—you go and get a newspaper.
Dolly (*suspiciously*) Why me?
Liz. I've got to finish off this office.
Dolly. Oh, all right.
Liz. Better leave that piece of paper with me.
Dolly (*suspiciously*) Why?
Liz. Well, you don't want it to get blown out of your 'and while you're crossing the road, do you?
Dolly. It won't. (*She tucks the paper into her stocking*) I'll keep it in me stocking.
Liz. Mind it don't fall out of one of the 'oles.
Dolly. What?
Liz. Never mind. Go on—'urry.
Dolly. All right. Back in a minute.

(Dolly *exits.* Liz *looks after her with contempt*)

Liz. So 'arf of seven 'undred is three' undred, is it? Not if I know it, it ain't. (*She crosses to the telephone, lifts the receiver and dials, speaking as she dials each figure*) W-H-I-one-two-one-two. (*She waits*) Serve 'er right. The double-crossing . . . (*Into the telephone*) Oh, 'ullo. Who are you? . . .

THE CLEAN UP

That's right, I want you . . . Me? My name is Fumblepenny . . . Lizzie Fumblepenny . . . No. F for fried-fish . . . 'Ere, listen . . . I know something, I do . . . Now, don't you get fresh with me, young man . . . Well, if you listen I'll tell you. I know 'oo bust into the Millibank office . . . All right, then. 'Urry up and put me through to the sergeant in charge of the case. (*She waits*) Lot of slowcoaches. Couldn't catch their own grandmothers. (*Into the telephone*) 'Ullo . . . Yes—yes, that's right . . . Well, I know 'oo did it . . . I'm the office cleaner and I'd 'ave you know that what I don't know about what goes on in this 'ere office . . . Eh? . . . It's an important clue typed on a saucy bit of pink paper. It's in code but I know what it means . . . All right, I'll read it. (*She quotes*) "The quick brown fox jumps over the lazy dog" . . . Eh? . . . What do you mean, "That's nothing"? . . . It's what? . . . A typing exercise . . . Got every letter in the alphabet in it? So it wasn't 'im and his blonde secertry? . . . You've what? . . . You've already made an arrest. Oh, well, I'm sorry to have troubled you . . . Thank you, sergeant—and the same to you. (*She replaces the receiver. Forlornly*) Typing exercise!

(DOLLY *enters. She carries a newspaper*)

DOLLY (*crossing to* L *of Liz*) There's nothing in the paper about it. (*She hands the paper to Liz*) Another threehalfpence down the drain.

LIZ. I expect they're keeping it quiet.

DOLLY (*brightly and with a plan in view*) Finished the office yet?

LIZ. You know I 'aven't.

DOLLY. Tell you what, dear, I'll do it for you.

LIZ (*suspiciously*) You'll do what?

DOLLY. I'll do it for you. There! You get your hat and coat and 'ave a break. Go right 'ome and 'ave a cuppa.

LIZ. What 'ave I done to deserve such treatment?

DOLLY. Well, you know what a friendly nature I've got.

LIZ (*realizing Dolly's intentions*) Thanks, Doll. You won't forget to empty the waste-paper baskets?

DOLLY. I'll remember.
LIZ. And give the passage the once-over—promise?
DOLLY. Cross me 'eart. (*She pushes* LIZ *towards the door*) Leave it to me. Ta, ta!
LIZ. Ta, ta!

(LIZ *exits.* DOLLY *crosses to the desk, takes the piece of pink paper from her stocking, gives a quick furtive look towards the door, then lifts the telephone receiver and dials a number*)

DOLLY (*into the telephone*) 'Ullo . . . 'Ullo . . . (*Fiercely*) *'Ullo* . . . (*With a quick change of voice*) Oh! Is that Whitehall one-two-one-two?

(*The door quietly opens and* LIZ *enters. She wears her hat, coat and a feather boa. She stands by the door, listening*)

I said Whitehall one-two-one-two . . . Scotland Yard . . . I want to speak to someone about the robbery at Millibank's . . . Well, for goodness sake 'urry up and let me speak to 'im . . .
LIZ. Ta, ta! Give my love to the sergeant.

DOLLY, *open-mouthed, turns slowly and looks at* LIZ, *who exits as—*

the CURTAIN *falls*

FURNITURE AND PROPERTY PLOT

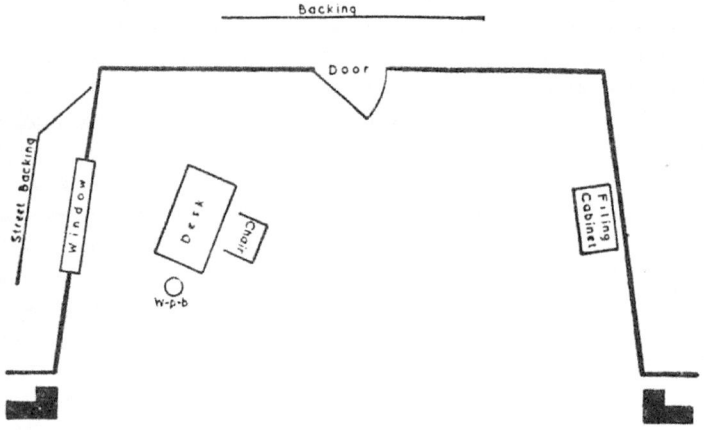

On stage: Desk. *On it:* typewriter, telephone, filing basket with copy letters on pink paper, pencil
Desk chair
Waste-paper basket. *In it:* discarded papers, pink copy letter with typing
Filing cabinet
Other dressing as desired

Set down C: Bucket of dirty water
Floor cloth
Scrubbing brush

Off stage: Newspaper (DOLLY)

LIGHTING PLOT

Fittings required—none

    Interior. Morning
    THE APPARENT SOURCE OF LIGHT is a window R
    THE MAIN ACTING AREA is C

To open: Effect of morning sunshine

No cues

TRYING TO TAKE THINGS QUIETLY

CHARACTERS

BERT, a burglar
LIZ, his moll
MRS FORREST

The action of the play passes in the drawing-room of Mrs Forrest's house in Belgravia, during the small hours of the morning

TRYING TO TAKE THINGS QUIETLY*

SCENE—*The drawing-room of Mrs Forrest's house in Belgravia. The small hours of the morning.*
  The room is on the first floor and has a window C *of the back wall. The door is* R *and the fireplace* L. *It is an expensively furnished room with long, heavy curtains over the window. There is a console-table down* R, *a corner cabinet up* R *and a glass-fronted cabinet down* L, *all with a display of curios, old silver and other valuable "objets d'art". There is a sofa* LC *and an easy chair below the fireplace. Some good pictures hang on the walls. A table* L *of the window is set with glasses and decanters. At night the room is lit by a chandelier* C, *with the switch below the door* R. *Other suitable furnishings may be added at the discretion of the producer.*
  (*See the Ground Plan at the end of the play*)

When the CURTAIN *rises, the room is in darkness except for the flickering of a dying fire. After a few moments a lighted torch is thrust between the window curtains, the beam explores the room, then* BERT *cautiously enters by the window. He is unshaven, is roughly dressed and wears a cloth cap. He shines the torch around the room, then speaks softly over his shoulder.*

BERT (*in a hoarse whisper*) All right, Liz—come on. (*He moves down* RC)

  (LIZ *enters by the window, leaving the curtains slightly open. She is a young woman, flashily dressed. She carries an empty sack*)

LIZ. Everything quiet?
BERT. Yes—quiet as the grave.
LIZ (*moving down* C) I don't call that funny.

* See page iv.

19

BERT. 'Twasn't supposed to be. If my grave was as posh as this, I wouldn't mind popping off tomorrow.
LIZ. Bert!

(BERT *shines his torch around the room, lingering on the various "objets d'art"*)

BERT. Blimey—look at it! Must be a blooming millionaire's.
LIZ. Who does it belong to?
BERT. Some old dame. Don't know what her name is. Charlie gave me the tip-off.
LIZ. Doing his usual window-cleaning act?
BERT. That's right. Just comes round and offers to do the windows for half a dollar the lot, puts his ladder against the wall . . .
LIZ. And has a nice long look into every room to see what's worth pinching.
BERT (*laughing*) That's right—and they pay him as well.
LIZ. Charlie's smart all right.
BERT. Are you suggesting I'm not?
LIZ. Aw, come on—let's get on with it.
BERT (*grumbling*) I didn't want to bring you in the first place. Don't hold with women coming on jobs.
LIZ. I've been on your last three.
BERT. Yes, and what did we get out of 'em? Just a lot of clothes you took a fancy to.
LIZ. A girl's got to look after herself.
BERT (*with a grunt*) Well, you look after yourself while I look after this joint. Got the bag?
LIZ (*handing Bert the sack*) Sure—here you are.
BERT. Good—here we go. (*He crosses to the console table down* R, *picks up the first things that come to hand and puts them into the sack*)
LIZ. Here—wait a minute. Is that worth pinching?
BERT. To me, anything's worth pinching.
LIZ. That's why you're still a small-timer.
BERT (*indignantly*) Who's a small-timer?
LIZ. You are, Bert—and it's no use trying to kid me about it.

TRYING TO TAKE THINGS QUIETLY

BERT. Didn't I do that job up at Hampstead when nobody else would touch it? And didn't I come away with two sackfuls of stuff?

LIZ. You did—two sackfuls of knives and forks and cigars and that—when there was a genuine Rembrandt hanging on the wall for the asking.

BERT. Aw, don't keep on about that. How was I to know it was worth anything? Looked to me like it was painted with brown windsor soup.

LIZ. That's just what I mean—you don't select, you just take the first thing that comes to hand.

BERT. Well, I . . .

LIZ. Like you're doing now. You didn't even look to see whether that thing is worth having.

BERT. How can I see in the dark?

LIZ. Let's have some light, then.

BERT (*alarmed*) Here now, steady. Do you want the cops in?

LIZ. Don't be dumb, Bert. (*She moves to the window*) We can draw the curtains, can't we? (*She closes the window curtains*)

BERT (*grudgingly*) Well, all right, but . . .

(LIZ *crosses to the door* R, *fumbles around for a moment, then switches on the lights*)

LIZ. That's better—now **we can** see what we're having.

BERT (*nervously*) I don't like it—all this light.

LIZ. Ah, gwan with you. Come on, let's have a look round. (*She crosses to the cabinet down* L, *opens it and peers at the contents*)

BERT (*bitterly*) That's right—take your time.

LIZ (*taking an item from the cabinet*) Now, that's a nice piece. (*She looks in the cabinet*) That isn't. That's a might-be. Come on, Bert, don't mess about.

BERT (*crossing to Liz*) What do you want me to do?

LIZ. Sort 'em out, you big dummy.

BERT. What do you mean, sort 'em out?

LIZ (*impatiently*) Put the maybes here, the certainlys

over there, and the no-goods here. Come on. (*She passes various pieces from the cabinet to Bert*)

BERT (*placing the objects into three different piles; grumbling*) This reminds me of the time when I used to work in Johnson's Auction Rooms.

(*During the ensuing dialogue* LIZ *clears the cabinet down* L, *then deals with the corner cabinet up* R *and finishes with the console table down* R. *She hands the articles to* BERT, *who places them on the various piles*)

LIZ. Work? You never did no work—all you did was case the joint.

BERT. Yes, and all I found worth pinching was a grand piano.

LIZ. Here, you, this one. No, stupid—that's a no-good.

BERT (*sarcastically*) Don't mind me—we've got all night. And if we haven't finished we can come back to-morrow.

LIZ. Don't argue—here's some more.

BERT. Cor, strewth! I never worked so hard in all my life.

LIZ. Organizing—that's what you want, Bert. Here, take this. You sure there's nobody at home?

BERT. Been watching the place all day, haven't I?

LIZ. I hope so. Here. (*She hands him a vase*)

(BERT *drops the vase*)

BERT. Oh, sorry.

LIZ. I'll give you "sorry", my lad. Fortunately, that's one of the ones we don't want.

BERT. If we don't want it, what are we moving it about for?

LIZ. I told you—it's system.

BERT. It's daft, if you ask me.

LIZ. I didn't ask you.

BERT. All right, cocky—don't snap at me.

LIZ. I'll snap if I want to.

BERT. Yes—just like a bit of elastic. You snap and I'll do a stretch.

Liz. That joke can go on the "no-good" pile.
Bert. Oh, get on with it—you talk too much. If there was anyone within a mile of the place we'd have been inside by now. And another thing . . .
Liz (*interrupting; sharply*) What was that?
Bert. What?
Liz. I thought I heard something.
Bert (*disgustedly*) Just like a woman—losing your nerve already.
Liz. Listen.

(*There is a short silence*)

Bert. I can't hear anything.
Liz (*relaxing*) I must have imagined it.
Bert. Sure. Well, come on—let's pack this stuff up.
Liz. You pack it—I'm going to have a look round for some clothes.
Bert. Clothes!
Liz. Well, if I depended on you, I'd go naked.
Bert. Now, now—no need to get vulgar.
Liz (*moving to the door*) Back in a minute.

(Liz *exits, leaving the door open.* Bert *packs the objects from one of the piles into the sack*)

Bert (*calling*) Here, Liz—do we take the maybes or don't we? Liz—*Liz*.

(Liz *enters, looking scared*)

Liz. Sh!
Bert. Eh?
Liz (*moving down* RC) Sh-sh!
Bert. What's the matter with you—boiling, or **something**?
Liz (*scared*) There's someone here.
Bert. What? Where?
Liz. An old lady—asleep in the next room.
Bert. What! There can't be.
Liz. There is—I just saw her in bed.
Bert. Gwan—you're seeing things.
Liz. Go and have a look for yourself, then.

BERT. Okay.

(BERT *crosses and exits. There is a short pause, then* BERT *re-enters*)

(*Alarmed*) You're right, Liz—let's get out of here.

(LIZ *and* BERT *drag the sack to the window*)

Don't make such a noise.

LIZ. I can't help it.

BERT. Hold the curtain while I put it on the ladder.

(LIZ *holds the curtain aside and looks fearfully over her shoulder at the door, as* BERT *hoists the sack on to the window-sill*)

LIZ. Hurry up, Bert.

BERT. I am hurrying. This bag's heavy. (*He heaves*) Hup! Oh, Gawd!

LIZ (*alarmed*) What've you done?

BERT. I've knocked the ladder down.

LIZ (*fearfully*) You haven't! You stupid fool!

BERT. Now, now—take it easy.

LIZ (*angrily*) What do you mean, take it easy—we're trapped.

BERT (*contemptuously*) Aw, don't be silly!

LIZ. We are, I tell you.

BERT (*jeering*) Windy!

LIZ. What are we going to do?

BERT. Do, my pretty? What do you think we're going to do? Fly out of the window—like Peter Pan.

LIZ (*worried*) Bert . . .

BERT. What's the matter? Don't you believe in fairies?

LIZ. Bert.

BERT (*irritably*) What *is* it?

LIZ. There's no way out of here—except through her room.

BERT. Oh, don't be silly—there must be.

LIZ. There isn't.

BERT. All right—so what? We'll go out that way.

LIZ. Suppose she wakes up?

BERT. Suppose she does? I'll just say "boo" to her.

Liz. She looked pretty frail to me. If you frighten her, she'll drop down dead.
Bert (*uneasily*) Well, perhaps we won't wake her.
Liz. Bert—I don't like it. If she pegs out—we're for it.
Bert (*biting his lip*) Well, we'll have to take the chance—we can't stay here for the rest of our lives.
Liz. Can't we get out of the window?
Bert. No—it's a sheer drop.
Liz (*shuddering*) Don't talk about drops to me.
Bert. Well, come on—let's chance it. Quiet, now.
Liz (*indicating the sack*) What about the stuff?
Bert (*regretfully*) Seems a pity not to take it. Lend me a hand.
Liz. Leave it, Bert—let's get out of here.
Bert. Cor, stone me! I'll never bring you on another job. I'll take it—you put the light out. (*He hoists the sack on to his shoulder*)

(Liz *crosses to the door, switches off the light and opens the door*)

(*He crosses to the door, stumbles and drops the sack with an awful crash*) Ow!
Liz. Bert! What're you doing?
Bert (*sourly*) What do you think I'm doing—playing Humpty Dumpty? (*He struggles to a sitting position*)
Liz. Bert—get up, for heaven's sake.
Bert. I will if you'll lend a hand.

(Liz *crosses to Bert.*
As she does so, Mrs Forrest *enters and switches on the lights. She is a frail, white-haired old lady, and wears a dressing-gown with a shawl around her shoulders*)

Mrs Forrest. Can I help? (*She crosses to Bert and helps him to his feet*)

(Bert *and* Liz *look in alarm at Mrs Forrest*)

There now—sit down and rest for a moment. That was a nasty tumble. (*She leads* Bert *to the easy chair down* L) Do you feel all right?
Bert (*sitting*) Y-y-yes, I—I'm all right.

Mrs Forrest (*moving to the table up* L) Here—have a drop of this. (*She pours a whisky and soda. To Liz*) Care for a snifter?

Liz. N-n-no, thanks.

Mrs Forrest (*moving with the drink to Bert*) Well, you might as well sit down, anyway. (*She hands the drink to Bert*)

(Liz, *staring at Mrs Forrest, crosses and sits on the sofa*)

Bert (*stammering*) Are—are you all right? (*He drinks, draining the glass*)

Mrs Forrest. Me? Yes, I'm fine. Why shouldn't I be?

Bert. Not nervous, or anything?

Mrs Forrest (*laughing*) Good gracious, no. Another drink?

Bert. N-n-no, thanks.

Mrs Forrest. Just as you like. (*She takes the glass from Bert and puts it on the table up* L) Well, let's have a look at it. (*She crosses to the sack and empties it on to the floor*) Mm—you missed all the best stuff. Did I interrupt you?

Bert. N-n-no.

Mrs Forrest (*pointing to the other piles*) What's all that?

Liz. Well—the maybes and the no-goods.

Mrs Forrest. Oh, I see—system. Well, system's all right, providing you know what you're doing. (*She picks up a piece from one of the piles*) For instance, this is more valuable than all that lot you were taking. Easier to get rid of, too. (*She shakes her head*) I'm afraid you're not very efficient—either of you. Did you have a go at the safe? (*She puts the object on the console table*)

Bert. Safe?

Mrs Forrest. Yes—here. (*She leans over the console table, moves the picture above it to one side, and displays the door of a small safe concealed in the wall*) It's an easy one, too. Did you bring any soup?

Bert. Soup?

Mrs Forrest (*impatiently*) Yes, soup—nitro-glycerine.

Bert. No, I'm afraid we didn't.

Mrs Forrest (*disgusted*) Well, really—you **are a pair.** Didn't you even know the safe was there?

BERT. No.

MRS FORREST (*crossing to* C) You didn't? Well, didn't you case the joint?

BERT. Well, Charlie did—when he cleaned the windows.

MRS FORREST (*chuckling*) I *thought* he was having a butcher's. He did the windows so badly. But you can't case a joint properly from the outside. (*To Liz*) Why didn't you do it?

LIZ. Me?

MRS FORREST. Yes—you could have got a job here as a charwoman or something.

LIZ (*indignantly*) Me—a charwoman!

MRS FORREST. Only temporary, my dear—and only in the interests of business. What about dabs—did you look after those?

BERT. Dabs?

MRS FORREST. Fingerprints. Did you wear gloves?

BERT. No—I'm afraid we didn't.

MRS FORREST (*shaking her head*) Dear, dear—you were careless, weren't you? I suppose you've been on the hook?

BERT. On the hook?

MRS FORREST. Clinked, jugged, booked, up the river, over the moon.

BERT. Oh, you mean "inside".

MRS FORREST. Well, have you?

BERT. Yes.

MRS FORREST. Then they'd have your dabs, you dope. (*In disgust*) Honestly, I don't know what the business is coming to these days.

BERT. What business?

MRS FORREST. *Our* business, stupid.

LIZ. Do you mean to say that *you* . . . ?

MRS FORREST. I suppose you thought that I was just a frightened old lady who'd drop dead with heart failure if she even saw a burglar.

BERT. Well, we did, rather. As we're all buddies together—I'm Bert Brown and this is my associate, Liz Wrenn.

Mrs Forrest. Bless your innocent hearts. Did you ever hear of Big Bill Watson?
Bert (*awed*) The bloke what did fifteen places in one night?
Mrs Forrest. That's the chap.
Bert. I've heard of him—one of the real big-timers.
Mrs Forrest. Many's the evening he's sat in that very chair you're sitting in.
Bert. Do you mean to say that *you* . . . ?
Mrs Forrest. And Flash Alf—did you ever meet Flash Alf? The best dip in the business.
Bert. Well, I've only heard of him. I don't mix with pick-pockets—not even the top ones.
Mrs Forrest. Ah, that's where you make a mistake. You small-time crooks get in a groove.
Bert (*jumping to his feet*) Who are you calling small-time?
Mrs Forrest (*calmly*) You.
Bert (*crossing to L of Mrs Forrest; angrily*) Why, you . . .
Liz (*warningly*) Take it easy, Bert.
Mrs Forrest (*to Liz*) You're quite right, my dear. He should take it easy, otherwise he's liable to blow his top. Liz Wrenn, eh? Old Daddy Wrenn's girl, aren't you?
Liz. Yes, but how . . . ?
Mrs Forrest (*laughing*) How did I know? I knew Daddy Wrenn just before he did his lifer on the Moor. One of the smartest con men I ever met. I can't think how a girl with a background like that can get mixed up with—(*she indicates Bert*) small fry like him.
Bert. Now look here . . .
Mrs Forest (*calmly*) Well, you *are* small fry. What have you ever done except petty larceny?
Bert (*crossing to the fireplace*) I done a good deal. Do you remember that job at the bank in Swinham? I did that.
Mrs Forrest. By yourself?
Bert. Pugnose Harry was with me.
Mrs Forrest. Oh, Pugnose was in that one, was he? Big stuff.
Bert. And that's not the only one, neither. There was that job at Caseton—me and Pugnose did that one.

TRYING TO TAKE THINGS QUIETLY

Mrs Forrest (*impressed*) Really?
Bert. Yes, really. And I'll tell you another thing. The slops have been looking for Percy Aston for months, haven't they?
Mrs Forrest. Percy the Penman?
Bert. That's him. Well, he's been hiding out with me—up in my attic. He's got all his treasury note forgery stuff there, too.
Mrs Forest (*admiringly*) Well, what do you know!
Liz. Bert—you're talking too much.
Bert. Nah—that's all right. She's in the business. (*To Mrs Forrest. Amused*) And to think I came here after your stuff! (*He looks around*) I suppose all this stuff is hot, isn't it?
Mrs Forrest (*modestly*) Well, not all of it.
Bert (*to Liz*) You see? Got it fixed up real comfortable, hasn't she?
Liz (*enviously*) Some people have all the luck.
Mrs Forrest. Oh, it wasn't all luck, my dear.
Liz. Did you ever go inside?
Mrs Forrest. Just short visits. To see some friends of mine.
Bert (*laughing*) She's a one, isn't she? "To see some riends of mine."
Mrs Forrest. Well, you know what they say—"Make new friends, but keep the gold".
Bert. "Keep the gold"! That's good, that is. (*He laughs*)

(Mrs Forrest *laughs*)

'Keep the gold"! (*He roars with laughter*)

(Liz, *somewhat uncertainly, joins in the laughter. Suddenly there is a sound of several police whistles off.* Bert *and* Liz *suddenly stop laughing.* Mrs Forrest *continues to laugh and wipes her eyes*)

What's that?
Mrs Forrest (*chuckling*) That? Oh, that's the police.
Bert }
Liz } (*together*) The police!

(Liz *rises*)

Mrs Forrest. Yes, I phoned them ten minutes ago.
Bert (*dazed*) You phoned them?
Mrs Forrest. When I first heard you getting in at the window.
Bert (*dazed*) But—but you're in the business yourself.
Mrs Forrest. Well, in a sort of a way.
Bert. But all those people you talked about?
Mrs Forrest. Oh, yes—I know them all right. You see, my son is Chief Detective Inspector Forrest of Scotland Yard. I know all the crooks.
Bert. But—but . . .
Mrs Forrest (*smiling*) I had to keep you here somehow, until my son arrived, didn't I?

(*There is a heavy knock at the front door off*)

(*She crosses to the door*) I suppose I'd better let them in. They'll bash the door down if I don't.

(Bert *makes a dash for the window*)

I shouldn't do that, if I were you. You'll only break your neck —and they're waiting for you outside, anyway. (*She stands by the door*) Oh, by the way—thanks for those tip-offs about the Swinham and Caseton jobs. Also about where they can find Percy the Penman. My son will be most interested. Much obliged. Oh, one last thing—just a little bit of advice. If you're going to take anything from a house, for goodness' sake learn how to take it *quietly*—as I'm *sure* you're going to do for the next few years.

Curtain

FURNITURE AND PROPERTY PLOT

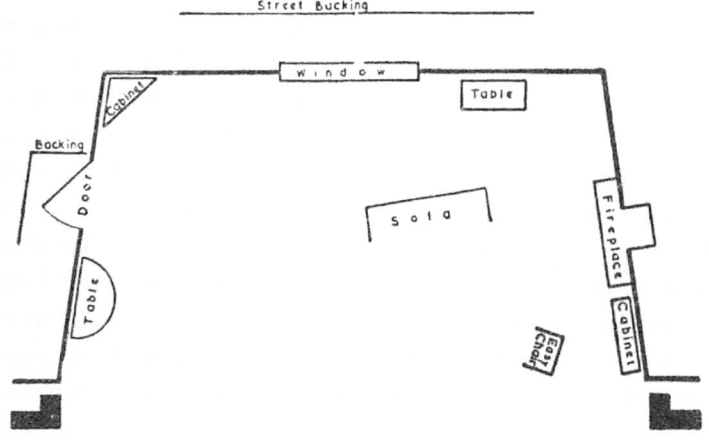

On stage: Console-table (*down* R). *On it:* "objets d'art"
Corner cabinet. *In it:* "objets d'art"
Table (*up* L). *On it:* tray with decanter of whisky, syphon of soda, 2 glasses
Cabinet (*down* R). *In it:* "objets d'art"
Sofa. *On it:* cushions
Easy chair. *On it:* cushion
Fire-grate
Fender
Fire-irons
Hearth rug
On mantelpiece: ormolu clock, ornaments
Over mantelpiece: mirror
Pictures on walls
Carpet on floor
Long heavy curtains for windows
Light switch below door

32 TRYING TO TAKE THINGS QUIETLY

    Chandelier (c)
    Safe door behind picture down R
    Other dressing as desired

Off stage: Electric torch (BERT)
    Large sack (LIZ)

Personal: MRS FORREST: handerchief

LIGHTING PLOT

Fittings required—Fire (practical)
    Chandelier (practical)
    Light switch below door R

  Interior. Night
  THE APPARENT SOURCE OF LIGHT is a chandelier C
  THE MAIN ACTING AREAS cover the whole stage

To open: Small flicker in fire L
    Blue outside window up C
    Room in darkness

Cue 1	As BERT enters Bring up general lighting a little	(page 19)
Cue 2	LIZ switches on lights Bring up lights to full Switch on chandelier	**(page 21)**
Cue 3	LIZ switches off lights Take out lights Switch off chandelier	(page 25)
Cue 4	MRS FORREST switches **on lights** Bring up lights to full Switch on chandelier	**(page 25)**

SCHERZO IN TWO FLATS

CHARACTERS

DOROTHY, a pretty young girl
MORTIMER, a not-very-bright young man
AUNT AGATHA

The action of the play passes in a corridor inside a block of flats, early one morning

PRODUCTION NOTE

In order that there should be no delays, both Dorothy and Mortimer should be "underdressed", that is, they should wear their complete change of clothes under their dressing-gowns, with towels or scarves to conceal their neckwear. The effectiveness of the sketch depends on Dorothy being very short and Mortimer very tall. This should be emphasized by heel-less slippers for Dorothy and elevators for Mortimer.

SCHERZO IN TWO FLATS*

SCENE—*A corridor inside a block of flats. Early one morning. The scene is a narrow one with exits* R *and* L. *There are two front doors, one* LC *and one* RC *of the back wall. The doors are complete with letter-boxes, bell-pushes and yale locks, and have adjacent numbers.*
(*See the Ground Plan at the end of the play*)
When the CURTAIN *rises, the stage is empty. Two full milk bottles are parked neatly outside the doors. That outside the door* LC *has a silver cap and that outside the door* RC *has a gold cap. After a moment,* DOROTHY *emerges from the door* LC. *She is young and pretty and wears a dressing-gown and mules. She peers cautiously out to see that nobody is about, then emerges fully. She stretches and yawns, sleepily rubs her eyes, then picks up her milk bottle.*

DOROTHY (*looking disparagingly at the bottle*) Skim—as usual. Hang that milkman! (*She is just about to re-enter her flat when she espies the bottle outside the door* RC) Gold top—full cream! Well, of all the nerve! (*She crosses stealthily to the door* RC *and exchanges her bottle for the other*) I expect he bribes the milkman. Serve him right.

(*As she speaks, her own front door slams shut*)

(*She crosses hurriedly to the door* LC) Oh, lord! (*She tries the door, but finds it firmly shut. She fumbles anxiously in the pockets of her dressing-gown, but without result*) Now what do I do? (*Again she rattles the door, hoping that it will open. Exasperated*) Oh, hang! (*She thinks for a moment and looks up and down the corridor*) Well, nothing for it. (*She crosses to the door* RC *and rings the bell*)

(*There is a short silence*)

Wake up, for heaven's sake. (*She rings again and waits*

* See page iv.

anxiously for a few moments) Sleeping like a horrible disgusting log. Or dead. (*She crosses to the door* LC)

(*As she does so,* MORTIMER *emerges from the door* RC. *He is a personable young man, clad in a dressing-gown. He is still three-quarters asleep, his hair is tousled and his eyes are half-closed. He fumbles blindly for his milk bottle, picks it up and re-enters his flat*)

I say . . .

(*The door* RC *closes*)

(*She crosses to the door* RC) Well, of all the . . . (*She gives a long ring at the bell*) Come out, you dope! Ungum those eyes and come out. (*She calls*) Show a leg there. Hey!

(*The door* RC *opens and* MORTIMER *appears*)

MORTIMER (*drowsily*) I've got my milk, thank you.

(MORTIMER *withdraws his head and closes the door*)

DOROTHY (*calling*) Hey!

(MORTIMER, *startled, opens the door. At long last it has sunk in that someone else is about*)

MORTIMER. Hullo—did you say something?
DOROTHY (*grimly*) I did—I said "Hey!"
MORTIMER (*at a loss*) Oh. Did you?
DOROTHY. You're a pretty heavy sleeper, aren't you?
MORTIMER. Am I? Yes, I suppose I am.
DOROTHY (*amused*) Heaven help your wife.
MORTIMER. Yes, heaven help her. I mean, no—I'm not married. Not yet.
DOROTHY. I shouldn't think you'll wake up in time.
MORTIMER. Oh, I can wake up, you know. Oh, definitely.
DOROTHY. Good. I'm glad. Because I want your help.
MORTIMER. Certainly. What can I do?
DOROTHY. I want to get into my flat.
MORTIMER. Oh.
DOROTHY. The door slammed.
MORTIMER. Oh.

SCHERZO IN TWO FLATS

Dorothy. My keys are inside.
Mortimer. Oh.
Dorothy. I can't get in.
Mortimer } *(together)* Oh.
Dorothy }
Mortimer. Bit tricky, isn't it? (*He puts his milk bottle on the ground outside the door*)
Dorothy. Very. What's the time?
Mortimer (*glancing at his wrist watch*) Just on eight.
Dorothy. Oh, good heavens—she'll be here at any moment.
Mortimer. Oh. Will she? (*After a pause*) Who?
Dorothy. My Aunt Agatha.
Mortimer. Has she got a key?
Dorothy. No. She doesn't live here. She's coming up from the country to take me out for the day.
Mortimer (*sympathetically*) Oh, dear.
Dorothy. "Oh dear" it is. Aunt Agatha is one of those people who get up at dawn and expect everyone else to do likewise.
Mortimer. That's bad, isn't it?
Dorothy. Bad? It's revolting.
Mortimer. Bit of a dragon, is she?
Dorothy. Dragon? She's got scales right down to the tip of her tail. *And* it's forked.
Mortimer. Probably that's why she gets up so early.

(*They laugh*)

Dorothy. If she finds me wandering about in the corridor outside my flat, in my dressing-gown, talking to a strange young man—I think she'll burst into flame.
Mortimer. That's what dragons are supposed to do, isn't it?
Dorothy. Yes, but if she goes up in smoke, so does my allowance.
Mortimer. Oh, I see.
Dorothy. By the way, since we're walking about here in our nighties, I suppose I ought to introduce myself. I'm Dorothy Neston.
Mortimer. I'm Mortimer Smith. How do you do?

Dorothy. How do you do?

(*They shake hands*)

Mortimer. Isn't there anyone in there who can let you in?

Dorothy. No. Just bachelor girl stuff. All on my own.

Mortimer. Not married?

Dorothy. No. No problems. Except how to get into my flat.

Mortimer (*thinking deeply*) Yes—now, let me see. (*A thought strikes him*) I know!

Dorothy (*hopefully*) Yes?

Mortimer. How about sending for a fire engine? They could get you in through the window.

Dorothy (*shaking her head*) Mm-mm—Auntie would be here long before that—then we *would* need a fire engine. I mean, if she found me like this.

Mortimer. She'd think the worst?

Dorothy. I'm afraid so.

Mortimer. Mm. Then we'd better get you inside.

Dorothy. How right you are. Go on—you're on the right lines.

Mortimer. Why don't you telephone down to the porter?

Dorothy. Because, my dear man, I can't get in to get to the telephone.

Mortimer. No, that's true. (*Suddenly*) I know! Why not use my phone?

Dorothy. Go on, then. I'll wait here.

(Mortimer *exits into his flat.* Dorothy, *smiling, lolls against the door-post, then a thought strikes her. She puts down the gold-topped bottle outside the door* RC, *picks up her original bottle and places it outside the door* LC.)

Mortimer *comes out of his flat*)

Mortimer. No go.

Dorothy. What?

Mortimer. My phone's out of order.

Dorothy. My lucky morning. Now what?

SCHERZO IN TWO FLATS

MORTIMER. I'll go down and look for the porter. You wait here.
DOROTHY. I can't stand about in the passage—someone might come along.
MORTIMER. All right—wait in my flat. I shan't be a moment.
DOROTHY (*doubtfully*) Well—do you think that's all right?
MORTIMER. Why not? As you say, you can't stand about here in the corridor.
DOROTHY (*teasing*) Suppose I steal all your possessions?
MORTIMER. You won't get very fat on those. Only some books, and one suit.
DOROTHY. *One* suit?
MORTIMER. The other's at the cleaners.
DOROTHY. All right—I promise to look after it. But hurry up.
MORTIMER. Okay.

(MORTIMER *exits hurriedly* R. DOROTHY *enters Mortimer's flat and closes the door behind her.*

AUNT AGATHA *enters* L *and crosses to the door* LC. *She is an elderly woman of fearsome aspect and wears a frightful hat. She rings the bell and waits for a few moments. As there is no answer, she rings again, then knocks on the door*)

AUNT (*calling*) Dorothy. Dorothy—this is your Aunt Agatha. Dorothy. (*She hammers on the door*) Wake up, girl—what's the matter with you?

(DOROTHY *cautiously opens the door of Mortimer's flat and peers apprehensively out at Aunt Agatha. She hurriedly withdraws her head and closes the door as* AUNT AGATHA *turns*)

Must be something the matter with her. Or else she hasn't come home all night—and I wouldn't put *that* past her.

(MORTIMER *enters* R *and stops short as he sees Aunt Agatha. He carries a ring with a quantity of yale keys attached*)

MORTIMER. Oh. Oh, hullo.

AUNT (*coldly*) And who might you be?
MORTIMER. I—er—I'm Mortimer—Mortimer Smith.
AUNT. You look like it. (*She turns to the door* LC, *knocks and rings the bell*)
MORTIMER. I—er—I don't think that's any use.
AUNT (*frigidly*) I beg your pardon?
MORTIMER. She's not there.
AUNT. How do you know?
MORTIMER. I—er—well, I mean, I don't *think* she's there.
AUNT. Young man—do you know anything of my niece's whereabouts?
MORTIMER. No—I mean, good gracious, why should I?
AUNT. That's just what I was wondering.
MORTIMER. Good heavens, no.
AUNT. Then how, may I ask, do you know she is not here?
MORTIMER. What? Oh—well—I—I—I think I heard her go out. Yes, that's it—I heard her go out.
AUNT. I see. How long ago was this?
MORTIMER. Oh, not long—a few minutes. (*An idea strikes him and he points off* R) Why don't you ask the porter which way she went?
AUNT. Yes. Thank you.

(AUNT AGATHA, *with a frigid look up and down at Mortimer, crosses and exits* R. MORTIMER, *making sure Aunt Agatha has gone, raps on the door* RC.
DOROTHY *opens the door and peeps out*)

MORTIMER. I say—your aunt's been here.
DOROTHY. I heard.
MORTIMER. I see what you mean about the scaly tail. I could hear it swishing.
DOROTHY. Did you get the keys?
MORTIMER. Well, yes—in a way. The porter wasn't in his office—(*he holds up the bunch of keys*) so I lifted his whole bunch of keys.
DOROTHY. Which is mine?
MORTIMER. I haven't the faintest idea.

DOROTHY. Then you'd better try them all.
MORTIMER (*crossing to the door* LC) Right. (*He tries one key after the other in the door, but without success*) Shan't be a tick—no, that's no good. No—how about this one? No. Never seen so many keys.
DOROTHY. Do hurry. I don't want Aunt Agatha to . . . (*She glances off* R *and sees Aunt Agatha approaching*) Oh!
(DOROTHY *scuttles into Mortimer's flat and closes the door.* MORTIMER, *unaware that she has gone, continues to try the keys, talking as he does so.*
AUNT AGATHA *enters* R, *crosses and watches grimly*)
MORTIMER. How about this one? No. Got to get this door open somehow. Come on, you brute, come on—open up.
AUNT. Young man!
MORTIMER (*turning; startled*) Oh!
AUNT. What are you doing?
MORTIMER. I—er—I—er—I was trying to open the door.
AUNT (*grimly*) So I imagined. Why?
MORTIMER. Well, I—you see—er . . .
AUNT. Young man, I'm beginning to have grave doubts about you.
MORTIMER. Oh, lor'!
AUNT. Do you know my niece?
MORTIMER. No. Yes. I mean—that is—I've just met her for a moment.
AUNT. Where?
MORTIMER. Here. I mean, in this corridor.
AUNT. Where do you live?
MORTIMER (*indicating the door* RC) In there.
AUNT. By yourself?
MORTIMER. Oh yes, definitely. I mean, absolutely.
AUNT. Then instead of hanging about out here trying to get into my niece's flat, I suggest you go in there.
MORTIMER. Yes, rather. (*He crosses to the door* RC, *then remembers Dorothy is there*) Oh, no—I mean, I can't.
AUNT. Why not?
MORTIMER. Well, I—I—rather like it out here.

AUNT. What?
MORTIMER. These flats are so small, you know—claustrophobia—I often come out in the passage and walk about.
AUNT. In your dressing-gown?
MORTIMER. Good heavens, no. I mean, yes.
AUNT. Young man—I think you're mental.
MORTIMER. No. No, I'm not really.
AUNT. You're sickening for something.
MORTIMER. No, I'm all right, really.
AUNT. I know the signs. Come on, now—in you go. I'll put you to bed.
MORTIMER (*alarmed*) No, I couldn't. Really.
AUNT. Nonsense! In you go. (*She moves to the door* RC, *pushes it, but finds it locked*) Where's the key?
MORTIMER. Key?
AUNT. Yes, the key. Come on—where is it?
MORTIMER. I—I don't know. It—it must be inside.
AUNT. I'm beginning to think you're not ill—you're a cat burglar.
MORTIMER. What?
AUNT. You just walk about corridors looking for flats to rob.
MORTIMER. No, really.
AUNT. And you put on that dressing-gown to allay suspicion. I'm pretty sure you're fully dressed underneath it. Let me see. (*She advances on Mortimer*)
MORTIMER (*backing away in alarm*) Stop—go away—help!
AUNT. I don't believe you live in that flat at all.
MORTIMER. Yes, I do. Honestly.
AUNT. Then let me see you go in there.
MORTIMER. I can't. I haven't got the key.
AUNT. What about all those keys you're holding?
MORTIMER. Which keys? Oh, these.
AUNT. Look like master keys to me. Come on. (*She holds out her hand for the keys*)
MORTIMER. Oh, no—I couldn't. I daren't. I mean . . .
AUNT. Stop drivelling, boy. Give them to me. (*She snatches the keys from Mortimer*)

MORTIMER. Oh.
AUNT (*examining the keys*) Now, let me see. Ah, this looks a likely one. (*She selects a key and moves to the door* RC)

(*As she does so, the door opens and* DOROTHY *emerges. She is dressed in man's attire, with a hat pulled well down over her eyes, and carrying a small suitcase. Without a word* DOROTHY *crosses and exits briskly* L. AUNT AGATHA *looks amazed, and* MORTIMER *is positively staggered*)

Who's that?
MORTIMER. I've—I've no idea.
AUNT. I thought you said you lived alone?
MORTIMER. Well, I do—but . . .
AUNT. Then who was that?
MORTIMER. The—the—plumber.
AUNT. The plumber?
MORTIMER. Yes, that's right. I remember now. My pipes wanted seeing to.
AUNT. I think your head wants seeing to.
MORTIMER. I'm beginning to think so, too.
AUNT. What?
MORTIMER. Nothing.
AUNT. Young man—is my niece in there?
MORTIMER. What—with the plumber? Good gracious, no!
AUNT. I'm going to see for myself.
MORTIMER. By all means—help yourself.
AUNT. I intend to.

(AUNT AGATHA *enters Mortimer's flat*)

MORTIMER (*to himself*) Fat lot of good it will do you—now. (*He calls*) Find anything? (*He moves to the door* RC *and speaks off*) That's right—look around. Don't forget under the bed—and the wardrobe. You won't find anything in the chest of drawers.

(AUNT AGATHA *emerges from Mortimer's flat*)

Satisfied?
AUNT. There's nobody in there.
MORTIMER. I told you there wasn't.

AUNT. You've told me a lot of funny things. But one of the things you haven't told me is why you were trying to unlock my niece's door.

MORTIMER. Well, I—er—er . . .

AUNT. Yes?

MORTIMER. I—er . . . (*An idea strikes him*) I thought I heard someone shouting for help.

AUNT. Good gracious! The poor girl might be ill or something. (*She crosses quickly to the door* LC *and tries several keys*) Why didn't you tell me, instead of standing there arguing? The poor girl's probably had a fainting spell or something. (*She unlocks the door*) Ah!

(AUNT AGATHA *enters Dorothy's flat.*

DOROTHY *enters furtively* L. *She is again in her dressing-gown and carries the suitcase*)

DOROTHY (*crossing to Mortimer*) Where is she?

MORTIMER (*pointing to Dorothy's flat*) In there. Where's my suit?

DOROTHY (*indicating the suitcase*) Here it is.

MORTIMER. You gave me heart failure—it's the only one I possess.

DOROTHY. What else could I do? I couldn't . . .

(AUNT AGATHA *emerges from Dorothy's flat*)

AUNT. Ah, there you are! Where have you been?

DOROTHY. I—er—just went down to get the milk.

AUNT (*pointing to the milk bottle*) But the milk's here.

DOROTHY (*blandly*) So it is—no wonder I couldn't find it.

AUNT. Well, don't stand about here, girl—come inside and put some clothes on. Come on.

DOROTHY. Yes, Auntie. But I . . .

AUNT. Here, give me that suitcase.

DOROTHY }
MORTIMER } (*together*) No!

AUNT. What?

DOROTHY. It—er—belongs to Mr Smith here. I was just bringing it upstairs for him.

AUNT (*to Mortimer*) Oh. (*She takes the suitcase from*

Dorothy and hands it to Mortimer) Well—here you are. Take it.

Mortimer *(grabbing the suitcase)* Thank you. *(He glances at his watch)* Oh dear—I shall be so late at the office.

(Mortimer *exits into his flat)*

Aunt. I think he's mad.
Dorothy. I think he's rather nice.
Aunt. The nonsense he's been talking—you wouldn't believe. First of all he said there was nobody in his room. Then he said there was a plumber.
Dorothy. A plumber?
Aunt. He *said* there was something wrong with his pipes.
Dorothy. So he's going to find out in a moment.
Aunt. What?
Dorothy. Nothing.
Aunt. Then I found him trying to unlock your door.
Dorothy *(pretending to be surprised)* Really?
Aunt. I don't think he's safe.
Dorothy *(moving to the door* RC *and listening)* He does seem to be muttering to himself a bit.
Aunt *(nervously)* I think we ought to go in.
Dorothy. All right, Auntie. After you.

(Aunt Agatha *enters Dorothy's flat.* Dorothy *knocks softly but urgently on the door* RC.
The door opens and Mortimer *peers out)*

Mortimer *(wrathfully)* Here—what have you done to my trousers?
Dorothy *(in an urgent whisper)* That's what I wanted to tell you—they were too long for me—I had to do something.
Aunt *(off; calling)* Dorothy.
Dorothy *(to Mortimer)* I must go. *(Apologetically)* I'm awfully sorry.

(Dorothy *crosses and enters her own flat.* Mortimer *emerges. He is fully and carefully dressed, and carries his hat* and umbrella. *His trousers, however, are cut off short just below the knees*)

MORTIMER (*with outraged scorn*) Women!

MORTIMER, *with a glare at the door* LC, *claps his hat on his head, and stalks off* R *in high dudgeon, his truncated trousers flapping about his knees, as—*

the CURTAIN *falls*

FURNITURE AND PROPERTY PLOT

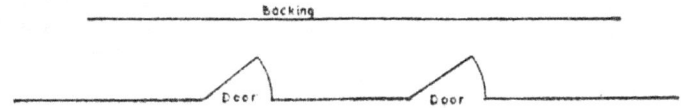

On stage: Fittings for two front doors: letter-boxes, bell-pushes, yale locks. adjacent numbers

Set: At door LC: full bottle of milk with silver cap
 At door RC: full bottle of milk with gold cap

Off stage: Ring with yale keys (MORTIMER)
 Suitcase (DOROTHY)

Personal: MORTIMER: wrist watch

LIGHTING PLOT

Fittings required—none

    Interior. Morning
    THE APPARENT SOURCE OF LIGHT are windows off R and L
    THE MAIN ACTING AREAS are RC, C and LC

To open: Effect of morning sunshine

No cues

FATHER'S ECONOMY DRIVE

CHARACTERS

GRANMA
MRS ETHEL SMITHSON
ANGELA, her daughter
GEORGE SMITHSON, her husband

The action of the play passes in the living-room of Smithsons' suburban house, one morning at breakfast time

FATHER'S ECONOMY DRIVE*

Scene—*The living-room of the Smithsons' suburban house. One morning at breakfast time.*

The room has a window c *of the back wall overlooking the garden. A door down* R *leads to the other parts of the house. The fireplace is* L. *A dining-table, set with breakfast for four stands* c, *with dining-chairs* R, L, *above and below it. There is a sideboard above the door* R. *Other suitable dressing may be added at the discretion of the producer.*

(See the Ground Plan at the end of the play)

When the Curtain *rises,* Granma *is seated above the table, reading the morning paper. She is a crotchety old person with a jaundiced view of practically everything.*

Granma (*reading an item on the front page with grim disapproval*) Disgraceful! They ought to be horsewhipped. (*She turns the page and reads another item with equal disapproval*) And *they* ought to be horsewhipped. (*She turns the page and reads another item, this time with quickening interest*) Mm—*they have* been horsewhipped.

(Mrs Ethel Smithson *enters. She carries a tray with a covered dish on it. She is a typical harassed housewife, aged about forty*)

Ethel. Morning, Mother. (*She puts the dish on the table and the tray on the sideboard*)

Granma. Morning. What's for breakfast? (*She lifts the cover of the dish*) As if I didn't know. You could smell them all over the house.

Ethel. Kippers.

Granma. You surprise me.

Ethel (*sitting* R *of the table*) Well, if you knew—why did you ask?

* See page iv.

GRANMA. Just hoping against hope. (*She helps herself to a kipper*)

ETHEL. Well, what do you expect with the price things are—peacock's tongues in aspic?

GRANMA. There's no need to be sarcastic, Ethel—just because I pass a perfectly ordinary remark.

ETHEL. Pass the toast, will you?

GRANMA (*passing the toast*) Aren't you having a kipper?

ETHEL. No.

GRANMA (*looking disparagingly at her kipper*) Can't say I blame you. When I was a young woman . . .

ETHEL (*interrupting*) Have you finished with the paper?

GRANMA. No. When I was a young . . .

ETHEL (*interrupting*) Give me the middle page, then.

GRANMA (*annoyed*) That's the bit with the fashion hints—I haven't read it yet.

ETHEL (*resignedly*) All right—give me the other bit.

(GRANMA *extracts a page from the newspaper and reluctantly passes the remainder to Ethel*)

Thanks. (*She rises, moving to the door, opens it and calls*) Angela—your breakfast is getting cold.

ANGELA (*off; calling*) Coming, Mother.

GRANMA (*studying her paper*) Doe eyes! Did you ever hear such nonsense.

(ETHEL *resumes her seat at the table*)

I'd give them doe eyes if I had my . . .

ETHEL (*studying her paper*) I see prices are up again. I really don't know how we're going to manage—it's bad enough as it is.

GRANMA. You'll have to economize, that's all. When I was a girl my mother kept house for eleven people on thirty shillings a week.

ETHEL. I don't see how we *can* economize.

GRANMA. Nothing simpler—you just don't spend so much.

(ANGELA *enters. She is a pretty young girl about nineteen years of age. She carries her handbag*)

FATHER'S ECONOMY DRIVE

ANGELA (*moving below the table*) Morning, Mummy. Morning, Gran. (*She puts her handbag on the table*) What's for breakfast? (*She lifts the dish cover*) Oh, kippers.

ETHEL. Now, don't *you* start, Angela.

ANGELA (*sitting below the table*) Can I have a piece of the paper? (*She helps herself to a kipper*)

GRANMA. Have you ever heard of doe eyes?

ANGELA. Of course. I'm wearing them—look.

(GRANMA *stares unbelievingly at Angela's eyes*)

ETHEL. That's one thing we *could* economize on—the amount of money you spend on make-up, Angela.

GRANMA. And be better off without it. Doe eyes!

ANGELA. What's all this about economizing?

ETHEL. We've just *got* to do it, dear—and that's all there is to it. Look at this. (*She shows Angela the newspaper*)

ANGELA (*reading*) "Cost of living index up three points." I never understand what that means, anyway.

ETHEL. It means we've got to economize. And that means you've got to give up spending all this money on cosmetics.

ANGELA (*indignantly*) What do you mean—*all* this money? It's only a shilling or two a week—and it's my money, isn't it?

ETHEL. Certainly, dear—but if you didn't spend it on make-up you could spend it on other things.

ANGELA. But I don't *want* to spend it on other things.

ETHEL. Now, Angela—you mustn't be stubborn.

ANGELA. Half a crown a week, that's all it is.

ETHEL. Half a crown a week saved is half a crown a week earned.

ANGELA. But, Mummy . . .

GRANMA. Doe eyes! I never heard such nonsense. Might as well paint the sides of your face grey and call it Elephant Ears.

ANGELA. Gran . . .

ETHEL (*rising*) I think I'll write all these things down. (*She crosses to the sideboard*) A shilling here, a shilling there. (*She picks up a notepad and pencil from the sideboard*)

GRANMA. Soon mounts up. When I was a girl . . .

ETHEL (*resuming her seat at the table*) If we could save a pound a week, that's fifty pounds a year.

GRANMA. Fifty-two.

ETHEL. Say fifty. (*She writes*)

GRANMA. Why say fifty? Why not say what it really is—fifty-two?

ETHEL. It's near enough.

GRANMA (*snorting*) No wonder you can't keep your accounts straight.

ETHEL (*writing*) That's half a crown a week saved on your make-up.

ANGELA (*indignantly*) Why pick on me?

ETHEL. Well, dear—it's got to come from *somewhere*, hasn't it?

ANGELA. If you're *really* worried about half a crown a week, I don't see why daddy has to have those gardening magazines—he never does any gardening, anyway.

GRANMA. Just like his father. When I was a girl . . .

ETHEL. I think you're right, Angela—that's a much better idea. (*She writes. To Granma*) Now, what are *you* going to contribute, Gran?

GRANMA. Me? Why should I have . . . ?

ETHEL (*interrupting*) I should think you could give up some of those sweets you're always stuffing yourself with.

GRANMA (*with dignity*) I do not stuff myself with sweets. It is not possible to stuff oneself with a quarter of jelly babies.

ANGELA (*to Granma*) You'd be better off without them, anyway.

ETHEL (*writing*) That's another shilling a week saved.

GRANMA. It is *not* a shilling—it's only eightpence——

ETHEL (*writing*) Near enough.

GRANMA. —and I don't see why I should be deprived of my one small pleasure. If you really want to save a shilling a week, why don't you get George to use spills instead of matches?

ETHEL. I think that's a very good idea. (*She writes*) Spills—a shilling.

GRANMA. And while we're on that subject, you'd save

a great deal more than all this if George just simply gave up smoking.

ANGELA. At least ten shillings a week.

GRANMA (*sniffing*) And the rest.

ETHEL (*writing*) Tobacco and cigarettes—fifteen shillings. Now, what else?

GRANMA. If you'd go down to the market you'd get the vegetables at least a penny a pound cheaper.

ETHEL. And spend twice as much on bus fares.

ANGELA. You *could* walk, Mother.

ETHEL. I don't hear you volunteering, my girl.

GRANMA. I reckon it'd be at least five shillings a week.

ETHEL (*thoughtfully*) Five shillings . . .

ANGELA. If Daddy didn't go to football on Saturday afternoons . . .

ETHEL. That would not only save five shillings . . .

GRANMA. But he could go down to the market and get the vegetables.

ETHEL (*writing*) Football—ten shillings.

ANGELA. *Ten* shillings?

ETHEL. Well, five shillings for not going and five shillings on the vegetables.

ANGELA. I say, suppose he doesn't agree to all this?

ETHEL (*with dignity*) It's not a question of agreeing, Angela. When economies have got to be made, they've got to be made.

GRANMA. How much have we saved so far?

ETHEL (*adding up her figures*) Two and six and a shilling and fifteen shillings and ten shillings—er—er—put down sixpence and carry nothing . . .

ANGELA. Twenty-eight and six.

ETHEL. Call it thirty bob.

GRANMA. Why call it thirty shillings when it's only . . .?

ETHEL (*interrupting*) Near enough. (*Delighted*) Why, that's—that's seventy-five pounds a year.

ANGELA (*thoughtfully*) Actually, if you want to know, it's—let me see . . .

ETHEL (*impatiently*) Oh, don't be pernickety, Angela—seventy-five is near enough.

GRANMA (*sarcastically*) I wonder you don't call it eighty.
ANGELA. Actually, it's . . .
ETHEL. Eighty pounds. Why, we could do all sorts of things with eighty pounds.
GRANMA. One of them could be to have that cistern seen to. Dribble, dribble, dribble—enough to drive you mad, going on all night.
ETHEL. I don't hear it.
GRANMA. People who sleep in the best rooms don't hear the things people hear who sleep in attics.
ETHEL. It is *not* an attic.
GRANMA. The ceiling slopes, doesn't it?
ETHEL. Only a bit of it.
GRANMA (*with great dignity*) I realize, of course, that beggars can't be choosers . . .
ETHEL. Oh, now, Gran—don't start all that nonsense.
GRANMA. All I hope, Ethel, is that when you're my age . . .
ETHEL (*thoughtfully*) Eighty pounds. We could have the front of the house done.
ANGELA. My room wants doing up, too.
ETHEL. I don't know that we can afford that, dear—we mustn't be extravagant, you know—just because we've got eighty pounds to spend.
ANGELA. Pity we can't save another twenty and make it a round hundred.
ETHEL. How much a week is twenty?
ANGELA. Eight bob. Or thereabouts.
ETHEL. I wish you wouldn't be so slangy, dear. Eight bob—er—shillings. Say, seven-and-six.
GRANMA (*with a snort*) Ha!
ETHEL. *Now* what's the matter?
GRANMA. If it's eight shillings, it's eight shillings. Why say seven-and-six?
ETHEL (*writing*) It's easier. Three half-crowns. There —one hundred pounds.
ANGELA. You haven't said what you're going to save the seven-and-six on yet.

ETHEL. Oh.

(*There is a double knock on the front door off*)

ANGELA. That's the post.

ETHEL. See what there is, dear, will you?

ANGELA (*rising*) Okay, toots.

(ANGELA *exits*)

GRANMA. Really, Ethel—I think you ought to do something about that child.

ETHEL (*vaguely*) Do something?

GRANMA. If I'd said "Okay, toots" to *my* mother, I'd have been put on bread and water for a week.

ETHEL. No wonder she managed to keep eleven people on thirty shillings a week.

GRANMA. It's all this going to pictures, that's what it is. (*She snorts*) Okay, toots!

(ANGELA *enters. She carries one letter*)

ETHEL. Angela—how much do you spend on pictures every week?

ANGELA. Not seven-and-sixpence, if that's what you have in mind.

ETHEL. Well, dear, I've got to save it from *somewhere*, haven't I?

ANGELA (*indicating the letter*) What about this?

ETHEL. What is it?

ANGELA. Dad's football pools. (*She resumes her seat at the table*)

ETHEL (*thoughtfully*) Yes, that's an idea, isn't it? (*She writes*)

(GEORGE SMITHSON *enters. He is a henpecked type with a drooping moustache*)

GEORGE (*crossing to* L *of the table*) Morning. (*He sits*)

GRANMA
ANGELA } (*together*) Morning.
ETHEL

GEORGE. Any letters?

ANGELA (*handing the letter to George*) Only your football coupons.

(GEORGE, *without much interest, opens the letter, glances at the contents, then puts the letter in his pocket*)

ETHEL. George—we've decided to have an economy drive.
GEORGE. Mm? (*He helps himself to breakfast*)
ETHEL. We've saved a hundred pounds a year.
GEORGE. Oh, yes? (*He holds out his hand for the newspaper*)

(ANGELA *passes the newspaper to George*)

ETHEL. It's wonderful what you can do with a little planning—a few shillings here, a few shillings there.
GEORGE. Yes?
ETHEL. Angela's make-up, for instance—and mother's sweets—and going down to the market to get the vegetables cheaper.
GEORGE. Very noble of you all, I must say.
ETHEL. Well, we've got to do *something*, George, haven't we?
GEORGE. Surprised to hear you're going without your warpaint, Angie.
ANGELA. I'm not.
GEORGE. But I thought your mother said . . .
ETHEL. I said we'd *considered* it, George. But we thought it'd be much more to the point if you gave up your gardening magazines. After all, you don't really *need* them, do you?
GEORGE. Well—if mother's giving up her sweets, I suppose I can go without my . . .
GRANMA. *I* didn't say I was giving up my sweets.
ETHEL. We thought that if you used spills instead of matches it would come to the same thing.
GEORGE. Oh.
ETHEL. That's not much to ask, surely?
GEORGE. I can never get my pipe going with a spill.
ETHEL (*triumphantly*) Well, there you are. Then you won't mind giving up smoking, will you?
GEORGE. I see. And would it be me who's going down

to the market on Saturday afternoons instead of going to football?

ETHEL. Well, you know *I* can't walk that far.

GEORGE. No, Ethel—I don't suppose you could. Although, if I remember rightly, when we were engaged you were the one who always wanted to keep walking.

ETHEL. George!

GEORGE. What else am I giving up?

ETHEL. Well, it did seem to us that these football pools are a complete waste of money.

GEORGE. Ah, now—I like my football pools. I get a lot of fun out of them.

GRANMA. That's about all you do get.

GEORGE. You never know. Here—tell you what I'll do. (*To Angela*) You give up your lipstick. (*To Granma*) You give up your sweets—(*to Ethel*) and *you* go down to the market—and if I win anything on the pools—I'll share it with you. How's that?

ANGELA. No, thanks.

GEORGE. Mother?

GRANMA. Certainly not.

GEORGE. Ethel?

ETHEL. Don't be ridiculous, George.

GEORGE. All right—just as you like. But don't say I didn't give you the chance. (*He glances at the clock*) Good heavens—look at the time. (*He rises*) I shall be late.

(GEORGE *crosses and hurriedly exits*)

ANGELA. I've just thought of something. We've made a big mistake.

ETHEL. What do you mean?

ANGELA. He's won something.

ETHEL. How do you know?

ANGELA. That letter was sealed. It's never sealed unless you've won something. Wouldn't it be just like him to trap us into refusing a share of it?

GRANMA. I thought he put that letter in his pocket mighty quick, now you come to mention it.

ETHEL. Well, of all the mean so-and-sos.

(GEORGE *enters. He wears his hat and overcoat*)

GEORGE. Well—good-bye all.

ETHEL (*rising; sweetly*) Oh, George...

GEORGE. Yes?

ETHEL. Did you mean that—about sharing anything you win?

GEORGE. Certainly—if you all do what you said.

ETHEL. Well, I'm willing to take the chance.

GEORGE. It's got to be for a whole year, mind you.

ETHEL (*swallowing hard*) I promise.

ANGELA. And me.

GRANMA. Anything they can do, I can do.

GEORGE. Well, that's fine. I'm glad you changed your minds. Now to show good faith, I suggest you all put the first week's savings on the table.

ANGELA (*taking some coins from her handbag*) Well, there's my two-and-six which I willingly sacrifice on make-up. (*She puts the coins on the table*)

ETHEL (*crossing to the mantelpiece*) Here's my five shillings that I'll save on vegetables and things. (*She takes some coins from a tin on the mantelpiece, crosses and puts them on the table*)

GRANMA (*taking a purse from her stocking*) Eightpence! (*She dramatically shakes her head*) No more jelly-babies. (*She takes some coins from her purse and puts them on the table*)

GEORGE. Good. I can see that you all mean what you said. It would have been a pity if you'd missed it.

ETHEL (*innocently*) Missed what, dear?

GEORGE (*taking the letter from his pocket*) Well, I've had a little win.

ETHEL ⎫
ANGELA ⎬ (*together*) ⎧ Oh, George, have you?
GRANMA ⎭   ⎨ Well, fancy that now!
                  ⎩ Really? I can't believe it.

GEORGE (*taking a cheque from the envelope*) Not a great deal—but worth having, I think. (*He hands the cheque to Ethel*)

ETHEL (*faintly*) A hundred pounds!

ANGELA (*rising; excitedly*) What! Let me see. (*She looks at the cheque*)

GRANMA (*rubbing her hands; pleased*) Well, if this isn't my lucky day.

ETHEL (*excitedly*) George—I'll start going to the market this very week-end. (*She kisses George*)

GEORGE. I take it you are all agreeable in appointing me official treasurer to this new family economy fund?

(*There is general assent*)

Good. (*He collects the money from the table and holds it in his right hand. He then takes the cheque from Ethel and crosses to the door*) Well, I'll cash the cheque and let you have your shares tonight.

ETHEL (*ecstatically*) Twenty-five pounds. Whoopee!

GEORGE (*stopping at the door and turning*) Oh, perhaps I ought to explain. That cheque doesn't *all* belong to me, you know.

ETHEL
ANGELA } (*together*) *What!*
GRANMA

ETHEL. But it's got your name on it!

GEORGE. That's right. But you see, Ethel, you've been nagging me for quite some time about the amount of money I spend on pools—so I've been having a little economy drive of my own. Instead of putting up *all* the money every week, I formed a syndicate down at the works—quite a large syndicate, as a matter of fact—me and ninety-nine others. So all I get out of this cheque is a quid—twenty shillings. I'll bring you your five bob home tonight. Good morning.

GEORGE *shakes the money in his hands, turns and exits as—*

the CURTAIN *falls*

FURNITURE AND PROPERTY PLOT

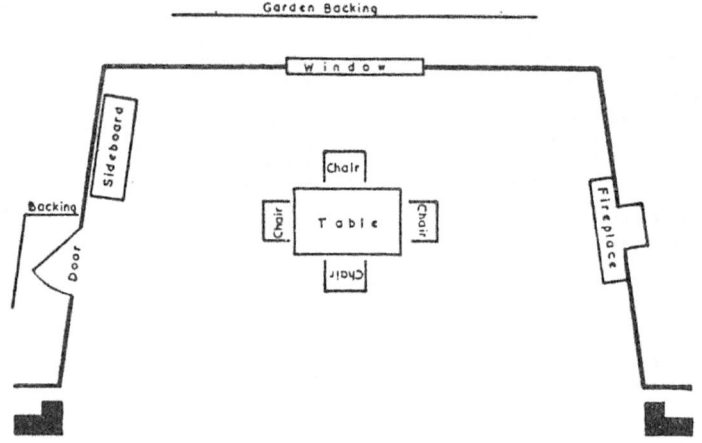

On stage: Dining-table. *On it:* white cloth, cruet, 4 each fish knives and forks, 4 small knives, 4 plates, rack of toast, dish of butter, tray with pot of tea, jug of milk, basin of sugar, 4 cups, 4 saucers, 4 teaspoons, dish of marmalade

Sideboard. *On it:* writing pad, pencil
Window curtains
Hearth rug
Fire screen
Fender
4 dining chairs
On mantelpiece: clock, tin with coins, ornaments
Other dressing as required

Set: On table c: morning paper

Off stage: Tray. *On it:* covered dish of kippers (ETHEL)
Football pools letter. *In it:* cheque (ANGELA)

Personal: ANGELA: handbag. *In it:* coins
GRANMA: purse. *In it:* coins

LIGHTING PLOT

Fittings required—none

    Interior. Morning
    THE APPARENT SOURCE OF LIGHT is a window C of the back wall
    THE MAIN ACTING AREA is C
To open: effect of an autumn morning
No cues

ART FOR ART'S SAKE

CHARACTERS

VALERIE
MRS CHUBB, the charwoman
AMANDA, Valerie's elder sister
MR CARVER, an art critic

The action of the play passes in Amanda's private den, during an afternoon in summer

ART FOR ART'S SAKE*

SCENE—*Amanda's private den. An afternoon in summer.*

This is an ordinary sort of bachelor girl's room. The door is C of the back wall and there is a large window L. The room is sparsely furnished with a divan bed R, a table RC, and an easy chair down L. There are shelves L of the door, littered with an artist's painting materials, tubes of paint, a palette and a jar containing brushes. A large easel stands LC, facing the audience. Other suitable dressing may be added at the discretion of the producer.

(See the Ground Plan at the end of the play)

When the CURTAIN *rises,* MRS CHUBB, *the charwoman, is on her knees down* RC *with a dustpan and brush.* VALERIE *enters. She is a nice young woman aged about twenty.*

VALERIE (*moving down* C) Oh, hullo, Mrs Chubb—have you seen my sister?

MRS CHUBB (*rising*) She went out just after lunch, Miss Valerie.

VALERIE. Where did she go?

MRS CHUBB. No idea, ducks—not far, I don't think, because she said she'd be back in an hour.

VALERIE. Oh, bother! I wanted to talk to her about our holiday.

MRS CHUBB. Haven't you done enough talking about that holiday?

VALERIE. Well, we haven't really planned where we're going, you know.

MRS CHUBB. Going to one of them foreign places, aren't you?

VALERIE. That's just it—and we haven't decided which. I want to go to Paris to see all the shops, and Amanda wants to go to Rome and see all the paintings.

* See page iv.

Mrs Chubb. Fancy going all that way to see paintings. Haven't they got any here?

Valerie. Ah—you don't understand, Mrs Chubb. According to my sister, nobody in this country can paint.

Mrs Chubb. Well, my 'usband did a pretty nifty job on the tool-shed a couple of weeks ago.

Valerie. That's not art for art's sake, Mrs Chubb.

Mrs Chubb. No, it was for the tool-shed's sake. If he hadn't of painted it, it would have fallen down.

Valerie. That's what I call *useful* painting—not like this stuff my sister goes in for.

Mrs Chubb. Ah, well—young women will 'ave their fancies.

Valerie. What do you mean—"young women"? Amanda's three years older than I am. About time she came out of the kindergarten. (*She looks at her watch*) I wish she'd buck up. I've got my hockey practice at four.

Mrs Chubb. Pity she doesn't do a bit of 'ockey practice, instead of sitting round here all day messing about with them pictures. I said to your mother only yesterday, I said . . .

(Amanda *enters. She is an untidy young woman, wearing an arty smock, floppy bow, and glasses. Her hair is untidy. She carries a large flat parcel about three feet square*)

Valerie. So you're back? I thought we were going to have a talk about our holiday.

Amanda (*placing the parcel on the table*) Don't talk to me about such unimportant things as holidays. (*She crosses and sits in the easy chair down* L)

Valerie (*indignantly*) Unimportant!

Amanda. I've just had a very great experience.

Mrs Chubb. Does your mother know?

Amanda (*ignoring Mrs Chubb*) The kind of experience one must have before one is really, fully mature.

Mrs Chubb. 'Ere, you're getting me a bit worried.

Amanda (*dramatically*) You wouldn't understand. Nobody would understand who hasn't an appreciation of all that's beautiful in art.

Mrs Chubb. Art? Who is Art? You don't mean Art Jones, the milkman, do you? Because if you do ...

Amanda (*interrupting; ecstatically*) Valerie, you don't know what a moving thing it is to come face to face, for the first time, with genius—genius.

Valerie (*in a matter of fact voice*) Well, come on—get it off your chest. What's happened?

Amanda (*with a far-away look*) Sunset on Wapping Creek.

Valerie. What?

Amanda. Sunset on Wapping Creek.

Mrs Chubb. That's what I thought you said. I've got a sister-in-law living down there. Suffers something 'orrible from the damp, she does. I said to 'er, I said ...

Valerie (*breaking in; firmly*) Exactly *what* is Sunset on Wapping Creek?

Amanda. Genius—pure, unadulterated genius.

Valerie (*disinterestedly*) Oh—a picture.

Amanda. Not *a* picture—*the* picture. And there it was —in that shop in the King's Road—just sitting there.

Mrs Chubb. Well, what else could it do—turn somersaults?

Valerie (*sternly*) Mandy—have you *bought* it?

Amanda. Of course—what else do you expect I did?

Valerie. Bought it? Actually paid money for it?

Amanda. Yes.

Valerie (*grimly*) How much?

Amanda. Not one fraction of its worth—not one decimal point of its glory.

Valerie. Mandy—*how much?*

Amanda. Twenty-five pounds.

Valerie (*horrified*) *What!*

Amanda. A fraction of its value.

Valerie. Where did you get the money from?

Amanda. What does that matter? I have the picture.

Valerie. Was it our holiday money?

Amanda. Holiday money? What do you mean— holiday money?

Valerie. You know perfectly well what I mean—the money we've been saving up for six months.

AMANDA. Half of it was mine, wasn't it?
VALERIE. Yes. But you know perfectly well mother won't let me go away alone. Now you've spent your half, it means I won't be able to go. Really, Amanda—you are the *end*.
AMANDA. But, Val—I couldn't *not* have it—I just couldn't.
VALERIE. Oh yes, you could've.
AMANDA. You don't understand. You've no *feel* for art. This means more to me than any holiday. To me it is the sun and the skies, the blue of the Mediterranean . . .
MRS CHUBB. I thought you said it was Wapping Creek.
AMANDA. The blue is the same.
MRS CHUBB. I bet the smell isn't.
VALERIE (*resignedly*) All right—so you've done in your holiday money on some blessed painting. I hope you go all pale and pimply.
MRS CHUBB (*indicating the parcel*) Is this it?
AMANDA. Yes.
MRS CHUBB. Bit big, isn't it?
AMANDA (*rising*) I bought a blank canvas—I'm going to spend the summer months copying the other one.
MRS CHUBB. Well, it's not my idea of a good time. Still, everyone to his muttons, as the butcher used to say.
VALERIE. Let's have a look at it.
AMANDA (*crossing to the table*) You wouldn't understand it.
VALERIE. Try me.
AMANDA. Oh, all right then. (*She opens the parcel and reveals a blank canvas*)
MRS CHUBB (*looking at the blank canvas*) Looks more like a snow-storm at the North Pole to me.
AMANDA (*standing the blank canvas against the divan*) Don't be silly—that's the new canvas. (*She takes a painting from the parcel*)
MRS CHUBB. Oh.

(AMANDA *crosses and puts the painting on the easel, facing the audience. It is just a patchwork of bright colours and looks like nothing on earth. It is about three feet square and can be clearly seen by the audience*)

AMANDA (*proudly*) There!
MRS CHUBB. Well, cor chase me up a drainpipe!
VALERIE. Is that really it?
AMANDA. Pure, pure genius.
VALERIE. Pure bunkum, you mean.
AMANDA. I wouldn't expect you to understand. You're a Philistine, Valerie—you've no soul above hockey.
VALERIE. Now, listen to me, Amanda. Are you pulling our legs? Or do you really believe that awful thing is good?
AMANDA. I think it is magnificent.
MRS CHUBB. But it doesn't look like anything.
AMANDA (*sorrowfully*) My dear Mrs Chubb—I'm afraid you're years behind the times. It's not *supposed* to look like anything—if you want an accurate representation of something, you don't use a canvas and paintbrush—you use a *camera*.
MRS CHUBB. Oh.
AMANDA. The *camera* is what *you* want—you just want things to look like things. The artist paints what he *feels*.
MRS CHUBB. He must've felt bad when he painted that.
AMANDA. Mrs Chubb—you're hopeless. But you, Valerie—after all, you are my own sister. I had the right to expect some feeling, some *nuance*, some *sympatico*.
VALERIE. I should've thought you had enough of all those in that horror. Really, Amanda, I do think it's about time you grew up.
AMANDA. Grew up!
VALERIE. Yes, grew up. Mooning about, swooning over a childish daub.
AMANDA (*with great pity*) Poor Valerie—poor little Valerie—I'm sorry for you. I'm sorry for anybody to whom art means nothing. How empty your life must be without art.
VALERIE. But that's not art—it—it—it's just a *mess*.
AMANDA. To you, perhaps. In the same way as

Beethoven, Mozart, Wagner would sound a mere *noise* to a Hottentot.

VALERIE (*angrily*) Don't you call me a Hottentot.

AMANDA. You wait until Mr Carver gets here.

VALERIE. Who?

AMANDA. Mr Carver. Not the sort of person you're likely to have met, Valerie—he's a very distinguished art critic.

MRS CHUBB. What's he coming here for?

AMANDA. When I phoned and told him I'd picked up a genuine Ignatius Winterbotham he said he'd come round at once.

MRS CHUBB. If that's what you've picked up, you don't want an art critic, you want a doctor.

AMANDA (*to Valerie*) You wait till *he* sees this—*he'll* know whether I've got a bargain or not. (*She crosses to the door*) Then perhaps you'll be convinced.

(AMANDA *exits*)

MRS CHUBB. Do you think she's sickening for something?

VALERIE. She's not sickening for it—she's caught it. And badly.

MRS CHUBB. Oh dear!

VALERIE. She's got an acute attack of highbrowism. Art for anything's sake except art's.

MRS CHUBB. How did he get back into the conversation?

VALERIE (*grimly*) And I've had about enough of it.

(*There is a knock at the front door off*)

MRS CHUBB (*crossing to the door*) Somebody at the door—I'll go and see who it is.

(MRS CHUBB *exits.* VALERIE *examines the picture from various angles, shaking her head. She turns the picture upside down on the easel, and looks at it again, her head on one side, but likes it no better*)

VALERIE. If that's great art, I'm Robinson Crusoe.

(MRS CHUBB *enters*)

Mrs Chubb (*excitedly*) He's here.
Valerie. Who?
Mrs Chubb. This art critic feller—Mr Carver—to see Miss Amanda.
Valerie. Oh, all right—better show him up here and let her know he's arrived.
Mrs Chubb. Okay.
Valerie (*suddenly*) No—wait.

(Mrs Chubb *pauses*)

Chubby—I've got a wonderful idea! Does my sister know he's here?
Mrs Chubb. No—she's out in the garden.
Valerie. Where is he?
Mrs Chubb. I put him in the dining-room.
Valerie (*quickly*) All right—leave him there for a couple of minutes—and lend me a hand. (*She takes the picture off the easel, puts it on the floor, then crosses, picks up the blank canvas and puts it on the easel*)
Mrs Chubb (*curiously*) What are you doing?

(Valerie *crosses to the shelves, picks up the palette and empties some tubes of paint on to it*)

Valerie. I'm going to put paid to this nonsense once and for all. (*She moves to the easel and begins to dab colours at random on to the blank canvas, in a wild design*)
Mrs Chubb (*uneasily*) Miss Amanda won't like you messing up her nice new canvas.
Valerie (*energetically daubing*) Messing it up? My dear Chubby—I'm painting a masterpiece.
Mrs Chubb. Don't look like it to me.
Valerie. To be quite frank with you, it don't look like it to me, either.
Mrs Chubb. But . . .
Valerie (*still daubing*) Look—this fellow Carver's no doubt just as bad as she is—he must be if he's come chasing round here—(*she indicates the picture lying on the floor*) to see that junk. By the way, tuck it out of sight somewhere, will you?

(MRS CHUBB *picks up the picture, crosses and stands it behind the divan*)

I'm willing to bet he doesn't know one daub from another. I know the type. They look solemn and talk about "an exercise in line and colour". All right—so I'm going to give him one.

MRS CHUBB. I don't get it. What good will that do?

VALERIE. Let him think *this* is the picture my sister phoned him about. Let him go into raptures about it—as I'm quite sure he will. Then let him—*and* my sister—know what a howling ass he's made of himself.

MRS CHUBB. Oh, I say—you are awful!

VALERIE (*standing back to admire her handiwork*) Dreadful, isn't it?

MRS CHUBB. Don't look any different from the other one, if you ask me.

VALERIE (*with mock severity*) I'm afraid you have no feeling for art, Mrs Chubb—it's *much* better. Go on now—fetch him up. And for goodness' sake keep my sister out of the way until I give you the tip.

MRS CHUBB (*chuckling*) Right.

(MRS CHUBB *exits.* VALERIE *adds a dab here and a dab there to her painting, then, hearing someone coming, she hastily replaces the brush and palette on the shelf. She then sits in the easy chair down* L *and assumes an innocent expression.*

MRS CHUBB *enters. She is followed on by* MR CARVER, *who is middle-aged, bespectacled, arty, and has an exaggerated manner*)

(*She grins*) Mr Carver, miss.

CARVER (*moving down* C) Ah, Miss Redcliffe—I understand your sister is out.

VALERIE (*rising*) Just for a few moments. Won't you sit down?

CARVER. Sit, dear lady? I haven't come to sit—I've come to look.

VALERIE. Yes?

CARVER. Your sister Amanda phoned me just after lunch and said she had something special to show me.

ART FOR ART'S SAKE

(*He turns and looks at Valerie's painting on the easel*) Ah! (*He moves to the easel and examines the picture, then moves down* LC, *and examines it from a different viewpoint*) Ah!

(VALERIE *exchanges a look with* MRS CHUBB)

VALERIE. You like it, Mr Carver?

CARVER. Interesting—*most* interesting.

VALERIE (*innocently*) I'm afraid I don't know much about art, Mr Carver—my sister is the artistic one in this family.

CARVER (*looking sharply at Valerie*) Is that so?

VALERIE. Tell me—what is it you find—er—so *interesting*?

CARVER (*gesturing towards the canvas*) The whole conception—quite remarkable.

VALERIE. It looks very ordinary to me.

CARVER. Ah, my dear young lady—you look at it with different eyes from me.

VALERIE. Naturally.

CARVER. You cannot spend, as I have spent, a lifetime looking at paintings, without being able to detect exceptional talent at a glance.

VALERIE. And you think this picture has it?

CARVER. Think, dear lady? I don't think—I *know*. There is a rhythm—a flow—an infallibility of composition. Surely you can see it?

VALERIE. I'm afraid I can't.

CARVER. Oh, come now—of course you can. *Anybody* can. (*To Mrs Chubb. Suddenly*) *You* can.

MRS CHUBB (*startled*) Who, me?

CARVER. Yes, you. Cannot you see the *genius* that lies displayed on that canvas?

MRS CHUBB. Looks like a lot of paint to me.

CARVER. Of *course* it's a lot of paint. But assembled with what skill. Look at the contrast of that colouring there—(*he indicates the painting*) with this here. Astonishing —quite astonishing.

MRS CHUBB. But it doesn't *look* like anything to me.

CARVER. It doesn't *have* to look like anything. **It's not** a *photograph*. It's a—a—how shall I put it?

VALERIE. An exercise in line and colour?
CARVER (*beaming*) Precisely!
VALERIE. It has soul, do you think?
CARVER. Oh, undoubtedly—lots of soul.
VALERIE. You think it is an expression of the artist's innermost feeling?
CARVER. Unquestionably.
VALERIE. You would say the person who painted that had quite exceptional ability?
CARVER (*laughing*) You understate it, dear young lady.

(AMANDA *enters, and stops short in surprise as she sees Carver. She does not at first see the canvas on the easel*)

AMANDA. Why, Mr Carver.
CARVER (*crossing to Amanda*) Ah, dear Miss Amanda. I kiss your hand. (*He kisses Amanda's hand*)
AMANDA. How long have you been here?
CARVER. Only a minute or two—only a minute or two. Your charming sister has been entertaining me.
AMANDA (*suspiciously*) Oh?
CARVER. We have been discussing art.
AMANDA (*superciliously*) Really? I'm afraid my sister is more interested in hockey.
CARVER. I want to thank you for asking me to come round and see this picture. It has been a very moving experience.
AMANDA. You liked it?
CARVER. Liked it? Dear lady—does a man parched with thirst *like* the vision of a limpid stream? Rarely have I seen such outstanding talent.
AMANDA (*purring*) Indeed?
VALERIE. So you think it's a masterpiece, Mr Carver?
CARVER. I certainly do.
VALERIE. Well, then I've got a little surprise for you—for both of you. *I* painted that picture.
AMANDA. What? (*She moves down* LC, *looks at the canvas on the easel and gives a strangled cry*)
VALERIE. Yes—*I* painted it. I just took your new blank canvas, Amanda, and your paints and I "painted"

a picture—if that's what you want to call it. Now, what have you got to say?

AMANDA. I—I—I . . .

VALERIE (*to Amanda*) Now what about all your talk about art and form and colour and all the rest of it?

AMANDA. But Mr Carver said . . .

VALERIE. I'm afraid he's no better than you, Amanda. There he was, thinking it was an Ignatius What's-his-name . . .

CARVER. Pardon me, dear young lady—not for one moment did I think it was an Ignatius Winterbotham—the style is completely different.

VALERIE. I'll say it is.

CARVER. I knew perfectly well that *you* had painted it.

VALERIE (*sceptically*) Oh yes?

CARVER. Certainly. I saw at a glance that the paint had only just been put on. Some on the canvas and some on your fingers.

(VALERIE *looks hastily at her fingers*)

VALERIE (*dazed*) Then—then—you were pulling *my* leg?

CARVER. Not at all. I meant every word I said.

VALERIE. But—but—I just dabbed the paint on any-how—anywhere.

CARVER. You may have thought so, Miss Redcliffe—but there was an instinctive talent guiding you.

VALERIE. But—but there *couldn't* be.

CARVER. Certainly there could. Why did you put red here—and blue there—instead of the other way round? (*He indicates on the canvas*) Why did you make this line go in this direction instead of that? No, Miss Redcliffe—you do yourself an injustice. You have a remarkable talent—untrained, of course, perhaps a little untrammelled, but none the less genuine. If the picture is for sale, I'll be very happy to offer a hundred guineas for it. (*He pauses*) You accept? Thank you. I'll send my cheque and my van round later this afternoon. (*He moves to the door*) And any more you do, please let me have first offer. Good afternoon.

(CARVER *exits*)

AMANDA (*furiously*) Well, of all the ... That *junk*! You call that a picture?

VALERIE (*calmly*) I'm afraid you have very little understanding of modern art, Amanda. This is what they call an exercise in line and colour. Let me explain it to you ...

She is still talking as—

the CURTAIN *falls*

FURNITURE AND PROPERTY PLOT

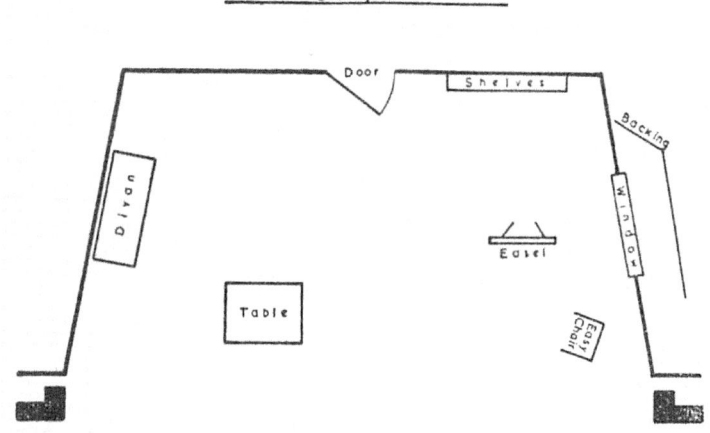

On stage: Easel
Easy chair
Table
Divan-bed. *On it:* cover
Shelves. *On them:* tubes of paint, palette, jar with brushes
Window curtains
Other dressing as desired

Set: *Down* RC: dust-pan and brush

Off stage: Parcel. *In it:* blank canvas, oil painting (AMANDA)

Personal: VALERIE: wrist watch
AMANDA: spectacles
CARVER: spectacles

LIGHTING PLOT

Fittings required—none

    Interior. Afternoon
    THE APPARENT SOURCE OF LIGHT is a large window L
    THE MAIN ACTING AREAS are C and LC

To open: effect of a summer afternoon

No cues

THE MAN WHO UNDERSTOOD
WOMEN

CHARACTERS

CHARLES } nice young men
ARTHUR }
EVELYN, a pretty young thing
MARY, a muscular young thing
AUNT AGNES
MRS GUBBINS, the cook

The action of the sketch takes place in the lounge of Charles' home on a wintry Sunday morning

THE MAN WHO UNDERSTOOD WOMEN*

Scene—*The lounge of Charles' home. A wintry Sunday morning.*

The sketch can be played in curtains. The minimum furniture required consists of two easy chairs LC *and a writing-table and chair* RC. *The setting may be more elaborate at the discretion of the producer.*

(See the Ground Plan at the end of the sketch)

When the Curtain *rises,* Arthur *and* Charles *are lounging in easy chairs in front of the fire, their feet on hassocks, drinks in their hands. They are idling away a wet and dreary Sunday morning.*

Arthur. How about going for a stroll before lunch?

Charles. What, in this weather—rain, cold, sleet? No, thanks.

Arthur. Well, we've been sitting in front of the fire for the past two hours.

Charles. And I propose to sit here for the next two hours—until lunch time.

Arthur. You won't find that too much effort?

Charles. After all, my dear chap, this is the day of rest.

Arthur. I'd be more impressed by that if I thought you'd done anything during the week.

Charles. I've been working on my novel.

Arthur. Ah, yes—the Great English Novel. How's it getting on?

Charles. Fairish.

Arthur. If you don't mind me saying so, Charles ...

Charles. As soon as someone uses that expression, I know it's going to be something unpleasant. Go ahead—don't mind me.

* See page iv.

ARTHUR. All I was going to say was that what I've read of it seems absolutely first class . . .

CHARLES. Except?

ARTHUR. Except the women.

CHARLES. The women? What's the matter with them?

ARTHUR. They don't live, old boy—they're made of cardboard.

CHARLES. Oh?

ARTHUR. They're not like real women at all. If you ask me . . .

CHARLES. I hadn't, but don't let that stop you.

ARTHUR. If you ask me, old boy, the trouble is you just don't understand women.

CHARLES. No?

ARTHUR. No. Now me, I've had a lot of experience with women. I understand how they work.

CHARLES. They're working now—getting your lunch ready.

ARTHUR. No, I mean how their mind works. Now, if you'll pardon me saying so—I don't think you do.

CHARLES. Of course I do.

ARTHUR. You don't, you know. Got a cigarette?

CHARLES. No, sorry—I've run out. You haven't smoked that hundred I bought you yesterday?

ARTHUR. No, of course not. But they're up in my room. But to come back to the point. The whole secret about understanding women is to make them do what you want. Now, I'm willing to bet that you're the sort of man who can never get women to do what you want them to do.

CHARLES. Nonsense!

ARTHUR. That's what you say. But can you prove it? Look here—let's have a little test.

CHARLES. How?

ARTHUR. How many women are there in this house? Four—Aunt Agnes, your sister Mary, her friend Evelyn, and Mrs Gubbins the cook.

CHARLES. Well?

ARTHUR. I bet you a quid you can't make those four

women interrupt whatever they're doing within the next ten minutes, and make them do something for you.
CHARLES. Such as what?
ARTHUR. Oh, any small chore. Not too small—otherwise there's no point in it. Not too big, because I agree that wouldn't be fair.
CHARLES. Well, what do you suggest?
ARTHUR (*thoughtfully*) Um—let me see. I know! You've run out of cigarettes, haven't you?
CHARLES. Yes.
ARTHUR. See if you can persuade any of them to go out and get you some.
CHARLES. What, in this weather?
ARTHUR. That's the whole point of it. Can you persuade them?
CHARLES. The shops are shut.
ARTHUR. The pub on the corner is open.
CHARLES (*doubtfully*) Mm.
ARTHUR. What's the matter? Don't you think you can do it?
CHARLES (*rising*) Of course I could—if I wanted to.
ARTHUR. Big talk, Charles. Big talk. I bet you a pound you couldn't.
CHARLES. Done. (*He shakes hands with Arthur*)
ARTHUR. I'll wheel them in here one by one and you can see how far you get. (*He rises*)
CHARLES. Okay. But no cheating—no telling them what's going on.
ARTHUR. Of course not. (*He laughs*) I can as good as feel that pound in my pocket.

(ARTHUR *puts his glass on the table and exits* R. CHARLES *ponders for a moment, then puts his glass on the table, hastily spreads the books and papers, ruffles his hair and sits at the table as if he is hard at work.*

AUNT AGNES *enters. She is an elderly woman of the "no-nonsense" type*)

CHARLES. Oh, hello, Aunt Agnes. I was just thinking about you. (*He smiles ingratiatingly*)

AUNT (*frostily*) Wanting me to do something for you, no doubt.

CHARLES (*shocked*) Good gracious, Auntie—what an idea!

AUNT. Well, what *do* you want?

CHARLES. I want you to allow me to do something for *you*.

AUNT. That's a change, I must say.

CHARLES. I want you to allow me to dedicate my new novel to you.

AUNT (*pleased*) Why, Charles—how nice of you.

CHARLES. No, no—just a token of my affection and esteem, dear Aunt.

AUNT. Is it finished?

CHARLES. No, no—as a matter of fact, it isn't. I'm stuck.

AUNT. Oh, Charles!

CHARLES. Just as I'd got the whole thing planned, the scene set, the characters on—suddenly it ground to a stop, and I haven't been able to move it an inch.

AUNT. I expect it will come out all right, if you just think about it for a while.

CHARLES. Auntie! You're so right. That's all it needs—some thinking. But, alas, I cannot think.

AUNT. Why on earth not?

CHARLES. I've run out of cigarettes.

AUNT. What's that got to do with it?

CHARLES. I need the soothing anodyne of tobacco—I need the peaceful touch of My Lady Nicotine.

AUNT. Well, why don't you go and get some?

CHARLES. No, no—that's impossible. While my novel —*your* novel—is in this fluid state I dare not leave it, not even for an instant. Suppose an idea came to me just as I was crossing the High Street—*the* idea—the idea that is going to make *your* novel ring down the corridors of literature—and I wasn't *here* to write it down? No, dear Aunt Agnes, in *your* interests I dare not leave this house. And yet my poor nerves cry out for a cigarette. (*An idea strikes him*) I know! Would it be possible, perhaps, that *you*, dear Aunt Agnes, could pop across to the *Blue Lion* . . .

AUNT. Certainly not.
CHARLES (*dashed*) Oh.
AUNT. I never heard such a lot of nonsense in all my life. "Soothing touch of My Lady Nicotine." Well, really, Charles—sometimes I think you take after your poor Uncle Willie who'd never wear shoes because he thought they were always sticking their tongues out at him.
CHARLES. But, Auntie . . .
AUNT (*firmly*) No, Charles. I simply will not pander to this weakness. If you can't think without acting like an incinerator, then it's time you gave up thinking.

(AUNT AGNES *exits* R.
ARTHUR *enters* L)

ARTHUR. Well?
CHARLES. No go. She wouldn't fall for it.
ARTHUR. Good! One for me. Look out—here comes the next.

(ARTHUR *exits hurriedly* L.
EVELYN *enters* R. *She is a pretty girl who is inclined to regard Charles as a "possible"*)

EVELYN. Hullo, Charles—still working?
CHARLES (*in a worldly manner*) Hullo, Evelyn, my dear. No—just contemplating.
EVELYN. Contemplating what?
CHARLES (*rising*) Ah, there are so many things one can contemplate. One can contemplate the scenery, contemplate a thought, contemplate matrimony . . .
EVELYN (*fluttering a little*) Charles! The things you say.
CHARLES (*moving to* L *of Evelyn*) They're nothing to the things I think.
EVELYN. I bet!
CHARLES. You know, Evelyn, you have a quality of making people feel *comfortable*.
EVELYN. Comfortable?
CHARLES. Yes. Relaxed—at ease—homely.
EVELYN. Oh, so I'm homely!
CHARLES. No, no—I didn't say that. But with a word,

or a look, or just with your very presence, you make me feel *at home*.

EVELYN. But you are at home.

CHARLES. In body, perhaps. But in mind . . . (*He shrugs*) A man needs something more than tables and chairs and carpets to make a home.

EVELYN. You mean he wants a good cook.

CHARLES (*laughing*) Oh yes, that. But something more. (*Romantically*) I see home as a place of relaxation, of comfort—a haven from the vicissitudes of life. A place to which a man can return at the end of a long day, certain that he will be greeted with love and affection . . .

EVELYN. What's the difference?

CHARLES (*thrown off his romantic note for a moment*) What?

EVELYN. Love and affection.

CHARLES (*taking her hand*) Affection, my dear Evelyn, is a warm glow; love is a blazing furnace.

EVELYN (*withdrawing her hand*) Oh yes—that reminds me. I came in to see if the fire wanted making up.

CHARLES (*laughing*) Evelyn—you have no romance.

EVELYN. Oh, Charles.

CHARLES. A pretty girl like you should be full of romance. Your pretty head should be full of dreams.

EVELYN. How do you know it isn't?

CHARLES. You should be preparing yourself for the future—for *your* future.

EVELYN. But I don't know what it is.

CHARLES. I do.

EVELYN. Oh, do you really? Can you tell fortunes?

CHARLES. I can tell yours.

EVELYN. Can you really? (*She holds out her hand for her palm to be read*) Well, go on.

CHARLES (*taking her hand*) I see here a marriage—two children—two pretty little children.

EVELYN (*giggling*) Boys or girls?

CHARLES. One of each.

EVELYN (*singing*) First a girl and then a boy . . .

CHARLES As a matter of fact, it's the other way round.

EVELYN. And then?

THE MAN WHO UNDERSTOOD WOMEN 89

CHARLES. Then I see tragedy.
EVELYN. Charles!
CHARLES. The home breaks up—the family disintegrates. Your husband does away with himself. The children are sent to an orphanage.
EVELYN. What happened?
CHARLES. "For the want of a nail a horseshoe was lost; for the want of a horseshoe a horse was lost; for the want of a horse . . ."
EVELYN. What on earth are you talking about?
CHARLES (*dramatically*) There was this happy family—a fine, noble husband, devoted to his wife and children. This pretty adoring wife—these two lovely children. But there was a flaw—a fatal flaw—in the wife.
EVELYN. She drank?
CHARLES. Worse. She forgot things.
EVELYN. What did she forget—to destroy the letters from her lover?
CHARLES. She forgot her husband was a man.
EVELYN. What an odd thing to do.
CHARLES. She forgot that although a man may willingly lay down his life for his wife and children, that a man has certain—well, let's face it—weaknesses. The average man places great store on little pleasures. It may seem unreasonable to you, a sensible woman, but it is nevertheless a fact that kingdoms have been lost for want of a horseshoe nail.
EVELYN. Are we back on that again?
CHARLES. This wife forgot one thing—that to her husband a Sunday morning without a cigarette was like a car without petrol, like an angel without wings.
EVELYN. I've got a feeling this is leading up to something.
CHARLES. Well, it does just so happen that I've run out of cigarettes.
EVELYN. And you want me to go out in the rain and get you some!
CHARLES. Well . . .
EVELYN. No.
CHARLES. Remember the home that was wrecked—

the two poor little children in the orphanage. Don't you think you ought to start getting into practice now?

EVELYN. If that entails going out in the rain to beg cigarettes from that dreadful barmaid at the *Blue Lion*— I'd sooner remain a spinster.

CHARLES. Evelyn . . .

EVELYN. *No*, Charles.

(EVELYN *exits* R.
  ARTHUR *enters* L)

ARTHUR. Yes?
CHARLES. No.
ARTHUR. Good. Another one to me.
CHARLES (*sitting at the table*) I'm beginning to think you've fixed these females.
ARTHUR. No, upon my honour, I haven't.

(MARY, *Charles' sister, enters* R. *She is a masculine young woman with a hail-fellow manner and a deep voice. She wears a blazer and carries a hockey stick*)

MARY. Who's that blabbing about on his honour? You, Charles?
ARTHUR. No, it was me.
MARY. I.
ARTHUR. Watch your grammar.
CHARLES. Hullo, old horse.
MARY. That's no way to talk to your sister.
CHARLES (*contrite*) No, sorry, Mary. As a matter of fact, I did want to have a word with you. (*He makes signs to Arthur to go*)

(ARTHUR *exits* L)

MARY. Well, come on—what is it? Get it off your chest.
CHARLES. Look here, Mary, we've always been pals, haven't we?
MARY (*suspiciously*) Well?
CHARLES. I mean, more like two brothers, really.
MARY. Only because I wanted it that way.

THE MAN WHO UNDERSTOOD WOMEN 91

CHARLES (*hastily*) Well, we have been, anyway. I've never treated you as one of the weaker sex, have I?
MARY. Not since I beat you at tennis, bowled you at cricket and wiped you up in the hundred yards.
CHARLES. Er—yes, quite. I think it was a jolly good show on your part.
MARY. You never said that before—you always said I cheated.
CHARLES (*with a forced laugh*) Oh, did I? Well, I knew what a sport you were, really.
MARY. Did you?
CHARLES. Of course. Sportsmanship—why, Mary, that's your middle name.
MARY. Well, I try to play the game.
CHARLES. I know you do, Mary. That's why I can tell you what I'm about to.
MARY. Go on.
CHARLES. I couldn't say this to anyone but you, Mary —but I know you'll understand. I'm in a fix.
MARY. What is it—women?
CHARLES. Frankly, yes.
MARY (*contemptuously*) Ah . . .
CHARLES. Well, you know how it **is**.
MARY. Who is it this time?
CHARLES. Flossie.
MARY. The barmaid at the *Blue Lion*?
CHARLES. That's the one.
MARY. Can't say I think much of your taste, old man.
CHARLES. She's got a certain kind of glamour.
MARY. She's also got a blue parting. When I was having a pint in there the other night, I noticed it most particularly.
CHARLES. Well, there it is. Just the heat of the moment and all that.
MARY (*alarmed*) I say, you haven't . . . ?
CHARLES (*shocked*) Good Lord, no.
MARY (*relieved*) Oh, well, that's all right, then.
CHARLES. No, but I *might* have. That's what makes it so difficult, you see.
MARY. Makes what difficult?

CHARLES. Going in there.
MARY. Do you have to go in there?
CHARLES. Well, if I want some cigarettes, for example—as I do now.
MARY (*laughing*) Oh, is that all? Well, that's an easy one—I can soon fix that.
CHARLES. Oh, Mary, will you? I say, that's jolly decent of you.
MARY (*taking a pouch from her pocket*) Have a fill of my shag.
CHARLES (*disappointed*) I don't smoke a pipe, you know that.
MARY. Pity. Might make a man of you.

(MARY *takes a pipe from her pocket, puts it in her mouth, then exits* R.
ARTHUR *enters* L)

ARTHUR. No?
CHARLES. *No.*
ARTHUR (*with mock sorrow*) Tch—tch! Well, now there's only Mrs Gubbins—I'll send her up.

(ARTHUR *crosses and exits* R. CHARLES *ponders for a moment, then rapidly tidies the books and papers on the table. He then picks up the inkstand and carefully spills some ink on the table.*
MRS GUBBINS *enters* R. *She is an elderly ex-nanny now cook-general, with grey hair and a worried expression. She carries a dish-cloth*)

CHARLES. I say, Mrs Gubbins—I'm terribly sorry.
MRS GUBBINS. Now what 'ave you done?
CHARLES. I'm afraid I've spilt the ink.
MRS GUBBINS. What a mucky tyke you are, Master Charles. 'Ere, let me mop it up. (*She crosses to the table and mops the ink*)
CHARLES. I'm terribly sorry.
MRS GUBBINS. Ah well—no great 'arm done.
CHARLES. Yes, but I hate to give you extra work with all you have to do.

MRS GUBBINS. You've bin giving me it ever since you was so 'igh. I don't expect you to change now.
CHARLES. Ah, I owe you a great debt, Gubby.
MRS GUBBINS. Well, now you mention it, there was that 'arf-crown last week.
CHARLES. I didn't mean that. I meant all your devoted service these many years.
MRS GUBBINS. You're not ill, are you?
CHARLES. Ill?
MRS GUBBINS. I never 'eard you talk like this before.
CHARLES. It's just come home to me, Gubby.
MRS GUBBINS. Bin a long time getting 'ere.
CHARLES. Do you remember when you used to dandle me on your knee?
MRS GUBBINS. I remember when I used to change your nappies.
CHARLES. Er—yes.
MRS GUBBINS. Proper young terror, you was, too. I remember . . .
CHARLES. Don't, Gubby—don't remember. Already I am too much in your debt.
MRS GUBBINS. That 'arf-crown . . .
CHARLES. I mean, in all the kindnesses you've shown to me. Why, I might have been your own son.
MRS GUBBINS. Nice little nipper you was. Bit pimply, but you'll grow out of that one of these days.
CHARLES. I only had to ask for something—and there was good old Gubby ready and willing to provide it.
MRS GUBBINS. Well, I don't know about that.
CHARLES. Of course you were. And you still are, aren't you, Gubby?
MRS GUBBINS. If you mean another 'arf-crown . . .
CHARLES. No, no—nothing like that.
MRS GUBBINS (*resigned*) Well, come on—what is it?
CHARLES. Would you pop across to the *Blue Lion* and get me some cigarettes?
MRS GUBBINS. Why can't you go?
CHARLES (*rising*) I've—er—sprained my ankle. (*He limps realistically to* LC)
MRS GUBBINS. Oh, dear—'ow did you do that?

CHARLES. Er—playing hockey with Mary.
MRS GUBBINS. You better let me 'ave a look at it.
CHARLES. No, really—it's nothing serious.
MRS GUBBINS. Then why can't you go and get your fags yourself? I've got the lunch to do.
CHARLES. Please, Gubby.
MRS GUBBINS. I can't do both. Which is it to be—lunch or fags?
CHARLES. Er—fags.
MRS GUBBINS (*sorrowfully*) Just the same as ever. Always thinking of yourself. What about all the others waiting for their lunch? If you'd said "lunch" I might have gone and got your fags for you—just as a reward. But you didn't—so I ain't. Now, if you'll excuse me, I'll get on with me greens.

(MRS GUBBINS *exits* R.
ARTHUR *enters* L)

CHARLES. All right—don't say it.
ARTHUR. It's not for me to rub it in, old man. But I did say you didn't understand women, didn't I?
CHARLES (*bitterly*) Yes, you did.
ARTHUR. Now, me—I *do* understand 'em, you see. I knew perfectly well you wouldn't get any cigarettes out of any of them.

(AUNT AGNES *enters* R *and crosses to Charles*)

AUNT. Here you are, dear. (*She hands Charles some loose cigarettes*)
CHARLES. Why, Aunt Agnes! I thought you said . . .
AUNT. I know, dear—but I couldn't bear to think of that beautiful novel getting spoilt for the sake of a few cigarettes. Now don't bother him, Arthur—he's got some important writing to do.

(AUNT AGNES *exits* R)

CHARLES (*putting the cigarettes in his pocket*) Well!
ARTHUR. All right—so you get one out of four.

(EVELYN *enters* R *and crosses to Charles*)

THE MAN WHO UNDERSTOOD WOMEN

EVELYN. I couldn't bear to think of those poor children in the orphanage. (*She hands Charles some loose cigarettes and kisses him*)

(EVELYN *exits* R)

CHARLES (*triumphantly*) Now what have you go to say? (*He puts the cigarettes in his pocket*)

ARTHUR. All right—so you're fifty per cent right. That still leaves me . . .

(MARY *enters* R *and crosses to Charles*)

MARY (*gruffly*) Here you are. (*She hands Charles some loose cigarettes*) And don't get mixed up with barmaids again.

(MARY *exits* R)

CHARLES (*delighted*) Three out of four! (*He puts the cigarettes in his pocket*) Now if only Gubby will come up to scratch . . .

(MRS GUBBINS *enters* R *and crosses to Charles. She carries a conspicuous cigarette box*)

MRS GUBBINS. Always spoiled you, I did. (*She hands the box to Charles*) 'Ere's your fags. There's only a few left, I'm afraid. All the others have had a go at it.

ARTHUR (*indignantly*) Well, of all the nerve!

CHARLES. What's the matter?

ARTHUR. That's *my* cigarette box!

BLACK-OUT

FURNITURE AND PROPERTY PLOT

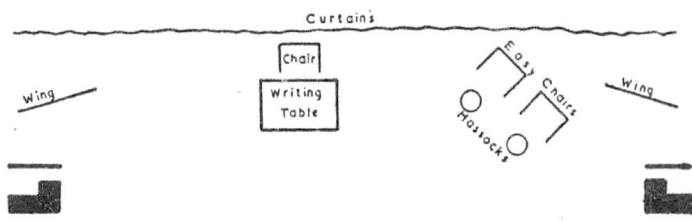

On stage: 2 easy chairs
2 hassocks
Writing-table. *On it:* books, writing-paper, inkstand, pen, 2 tumblers
Upright chair
Other dressing as desired

Off stage: Hockey stick (MARY)
Dish cloth (MRS GUBBINS)
Cigarettes (AUNT AGNES)
Cigarettes (EVELYN)
Cigarettes (MARY)
Cigarette box (MRS GUBBINS)

Personal: MARY: tobacco pouch, pipe

LIGHTING PLOT

Fittings required—none

    Interior. Morning
    THE MAIN ACTING AREA is C

To open: Effect of a wet wintry morning

Cue 1   ARTHUR: That's *my* cigarette box!   (page 95)
        BLACK-OUT